Jesus—the Life Changer

12 Bible Studies to Transform
How Teenagers Connect With Christ

·················· by Kelli and David Trujillo

Loveland, Colorado

Jesus—the Life Changer

····· 12 Bible Studies to Transform
How Teenagers Connect With Christ

Copyright © 2005 Kelli and David Trujillo

Visit our Web site: **www.group.com**

Credits
Editor: Paul Woods
Creative Development Editor: Kate S. Holburn
Chief Creative Officer: Joani Schultz
Copy Editor: Ann Jahns
Art Director: Toolbox Creative
Designer/Illustrator: Toolbox Creative
Cover Art Director: Jeff Storm
Cover Designer: Susan Tripp
Production Manager: Dodie Tipton

Unless otherwise noted, Scripture taken from the HOLY BIBLE, NEW
INTERNATIONAL VERSION®. Copyright © 1973, 1978, 1984 by
International Bible Society. Used by permission of Zondervan Publishing
House. All rights reserved.

When indicated, Scripture taken from *THE MESSAGE.* Copyright © 1993,
1994, 1995, 1996, 2000, 2001, 2002. Used by permission of NavPress
Publishing Group.

ISBN 0-7644-2875-6
10 9 8 7 6 5 4 3 2 1   14 13 12 11 10 09 08 07 06 05

Printed in the United States of America.

Table of Contents

Dedication

For our parents, Bob and Jeanne Blahnik
and David and Anita Trujillo, who have helped
us to see Jesus for who he really is: the Christ.

Acknowledgments

We'd also like to thank
...the youth group at Berthoud Evangelical Free Church;
...the students and staff at Covenant Christian High School;
...Dr. M. Daniel Carroll R. from Denver Seminary for your schol-
arship and inspiration;
...our fabulous editor, Paul Woods;
...Rick Lawrence for the opportunities to write for GROUP magazine and for all your encouragement;
...Dave Thornton, Amy Simpson, Mikal Keefer, and Kate Holburn
at Group for your friendship and for believing in this project;
...and Thom and Joani Shultz for giving us this opportunity to be
a part of your vision to help young people grow in their friendship
with Jesus.

Introduction

[Jesus] asked his disciples, "Who do people say the Son of Man is?"

They replied, "Some say John the Baptist; others say Elijah; and still others, Jeremiah or one of the prophets."

"But what about you?" he asked. "Who do you say I am?"

Simon Peter answered, "You are the Christ, the Son of the living God" (Matthew 16:13-16).

Seeing teenagers come to recognize Jesus as the Christ is the reason you do what you do. You're passionate about helping students move beyond a cursory understanding of biblical events into a thriving, growing, and life-changing relationship with Jesus. This resource will help you to do just that.

These Bible studies grew out of our own youth ministry in a small town in northern Colorado and were part of a year-long series David led that overviewed the story of God. Throughout the study series, we saw non-Christian seekers grow curious and look more closely at Jesus, saw students make first-time commitments of faith to Christ, and saw Christian teenagers' connection with Jesus deepen to a new level of love and commitment.

The 12 studies in this book follow the generally recognized chronology of Jesus' life. They'll help you lead teenagers through an in-depth and comprehensive look at Jesus, from the Old Testament prophecies foretelling his arrival to John's vision of Jesus as the Lion and the Lamb who reigns in the book of Revelation. Students will get a big picture perspective on Jesus' mission, his kingdom, his sacrifice, and his love. And they'll move beyond just acquiring knowledge; as they encounter Jesus, their lives will be changed and their hearts transformed.

Each study in this book lasts from **45 to 60 minutes,** and each one can be easily customized to fit your own ministry schedule.

At the start of each study, you'll find a **Leader Insight**—a section offering background commentary, expertise from renowned theologians, and notes on key Scripture passages in the study.

Each study launches with a **Connection** section in which teenagers will connect to the topic and with each other through games, discussions, movie clips, and other creative activities.

Youth will then dive into the **Exploration** section, during which you'll lead students through an in-depth study of Scripture. You'll employ a variety of study techniques such as inductive Bible study, the use of Bible research tools, the development of object lessons, and more.

Finally, each study concludes with a **Transformation** section in which students discuss and commit to application steps or respond to God in worship and prayer.

Every study includes an option that uses media—movies or music—to keep things relevant and exciting. These media elements are marked with a **Plugged In** icon. If you're unable to do any of the media ideas, don't worry—a non-media option is always included.

When you do use the recommended movie clips, remember that in general, federal copyright laws do not allow you to use videos or DVDs (even ones you own) for any purpose other than home viewing. Though some exceptions allow for the use of short segments of copyrighted material for educational purposes, it's best to be on the safe side. Your church can obtain a license from the Motion Picture Licensing Corporation for a small fee. Just visit www.mplc.com or call 1-800-462-8855 for more information. When using a movie that is not covered by the license, we recommend directly contacting the movie studio to seek permission for use of the clip.

Every student should have his or her own **Student Journal** at each meeting. The Student Journals contain content that kids will use in various activities in the studies. In addition, each week the Student Journal recommends several **On Your Own** ideas—activities and study suggestions for teenagers to use during the week in their own personal devotional time. By encouraging teenagers to do the On Your Own activities, you'll help them develop regular and lifelong prayer and Bible study habits. (If you need additional Student Journals, contact Group Publishing at 1-800-447-1070 or www.group.com.)

Jesus. He's the prophesied Messiah, the Word made flesh, the Son of God, the powerful miracle-worker, the Christ, the Anointed One, the Grace-giver, the crucified Lamb, the Resurrection and the Life, the Lion of the tribe of Judah, the Servant, the King...the Life Changer. Over the next 12 weeks, take off on the adventure of knowing him better. Your students—and *you*—will be transformed as a result.

Study 1

The Promised Messiah—Servant or King?

• •

Scripture Focus: Isaiah 1:2-4, 18; 7:13-17; 8:1-10; 9:6-7; 36:1; 37:30-35; 38:1-7; 42:1-4; 49:5-7; 50:4-10; 52:13–53:12; 61:1-2

Supplies: Bibles, Student Journals, pens or pencils, *Clear and Present Danger* video or DVD (optional), VCR or DVD player (optional), TV (optional), newsprint, marker, tape, ink pad, pad of self-stick notes

• •

> *"Who is he? What sort of hero approaches? What **is** this Mercy soon to be born among us? Why, he shall be a king!...[T]his King shall gather time and space into his kingdom, and shall himself embrace the history of humankind, for of his kingdom 'there will be no end.'"*
> —Walter Wangerin Jr., **Preparing for Jesus**

PREPARATION

Before the meeting, read the Leader Insight section to dive deeper into the topic of prophecies about Jesus. Then read through the study to familiarize yourself with the Scripture passages and activities.

For the **Connection** section, if you're going to use the optional movie clip idea, set up a TV and VCR (or DVD player) and cue up the movie *Clear and Present Danger* by setting the clock on the VCR to 0:00:00 when the studio logo appears. Fast-forward to approximately 1:08:15 when Jack Ryan and his wife enter the apartment.

For the **Exploration** section, tape a large sheet of newsprint on the wall.

For the **Transformation** activity, you'll need an ink pad and a pad of self-stick notes.

The book of Isaiah reveals two important aspects of how the Jews in the Old Testament thought about their faith: in terms of the past and in terms of the future. Looking to the past was important because it was a reminder of God's faithfulness to them as God's people. This inspired faithfulness in return, helping the Jews to live by God's commands. Remembering God's faithfulness led to righteousness and faith, whereas forgetting led to sin. This principle is emphasized throughout the Old Testament, and particularly in the Shema (found in Deuteronomy 6:4-9). In this passage, the people are instructed to love God with their whole being and to pass it down to their children, talking about it and putting symbolic reminders on their hands and foreheads as well as above their doors and gates. (Other important passages that emphasize this idea are Deuteronomy 6:1-25; 8:1-10; 2 Kings 17:38; and Nehemiah 8:18—9:38.)

However, Israel, like us, was predictably unable to overcome sin. Isaiah emphasizes this by pointing out that even dumb animals know and remember their master, but the Israelites had forgotten their God: "The ox knows his master, the donkey his owner's manager, but Israel does not know, my people do not understand" (Isaiah 1:3). Isaiah 1:2-6 is a basic summary of the sinfulness of God's people; this passage reveals that Isaiah is written with the primary purpose of addressing the problem of sin—the real enemy of God and his people.

This brings us to the second aspect of the Old Testament through which the children of God thought of their faith: the promise of the future. Isaiah introduces the coming of the "Anointed One" who would save Israel and the world from sin. This promise, found primarily in Isaiah but also described by several other Old Testament prophets, focuses on a future hope. As students

CONNECTION

Welcome students to the Bible study, and start things off by having teenagers form pairs. Explain that each person should secretly think of a new identity—the identity of a well-known person or character, such as a famous athlete, a politician, or a character from a favorite cartoon. Once they've thought of their new identities, explain that partners will ask each other "yes" or "no" questions to figure out the other's identity. Here's the twist: Instead of one partner interrogating the other, they'll both do the detective work simultaneously, asking each other questions back and forth, one at a time. The goal is for the partners to race each explore Isaiah during this study, they will discover more details of what that future hope looked like from the perspective of God's people in the Old Testament. As you lead this study, look to see how Isaiah develops the reader's anticipation for this "servant of God" by revealing partial but incomplete fulfillments in both Maher-Shalal-Hash-Baz and Hezekiah. Isaiah leaves the reader wanting and waiting for the truly "Anointed One," who will be both the king and the servant Isaiah describes. And so, despite the forgetfulness and sin of Israel, there remains a future promise of hope for God's people.

One more note may be helpful concerning the messianic prophecies found in Isaiah, especially if you're working with curious teenagers. When Isaiah offers his famous prophecy in chapter 7, he anticipates an immediate fulfillment of that prophecy in chapter 8 with the birth of his son Maher-Shalal-Hash-Baz. The same is true of his equally famous prophecy in chapter 9, where much later the "Prince of Peace" is personified in Hezekiah (Isaiah 36–38). But both of these fulfillments are strangely incomplete. It is certain that the author foresees a second more distant and complete fulfillment of these prophecies. This is clear by the way Isaiah organized his book. After Maher-Shalal-Hash-Baz seems to satisfy the prophecies in chapter 7, we read chapter 8, which offers additional descriptors. And then Hezekiah seems to meet these prophecies, until we find prophecies of the servant in Isaiah 42 and following. Beautifully designed, all three of these prophecies concerning a messiah (chapters 7, 9, 42, and following) point to a single figure beyond the scope of Isaiah. It is not until Luke 4:18-21 that we find the ultimate fulfillment in the person of Jesus. This "double fulfillment" concept of Old Testament prophecy is intentional and unmistakable.

other to see who can guess the other's identity first. This will be somewhat confusing (and entertaining) as teenagers continually switch back and forth between the roles of asking questions and answering them. Caution teenagers that they only get two chances to guess their partner's identity, so they'd better be pretty certain before they make a guess!

If you have time, allow students to switch partners and play several rounds of this game. When they're done, gather teenagers back together and ask:

- **What strategies did you use to narrow down the identity of your partner?**

- **What types of questions were most useful in helping you discover the answer?**
- **What are some situations in life in which you must be a detective, using questions and clues to help you discover what you're looking for?**

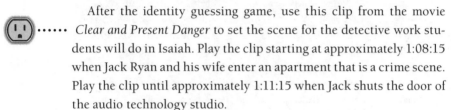

After the identity guessing game, use this clip from the movie *Clear and Present Danger* to set the scene for the detective work students will do in Isaiah. Play the clip starting at approximately 1:08:15 when Jack Ryan and his wife enter an apartment that is a crime scene. Play the clip until approximately 1:11:15 when Jack shuts the door of the audio technology studio.

This scene gives just a glimpse of detective work in action as the police try to determine the identity of a man wanted for murder. Luckily, the suspect left a recording of his voice on the victim's answering machine, and Ryan has the voice analyzed to determine the man's identity.

NON-MEDIA OPTION
If you're unable to play the video, just continue with the discussion outlined below.

Ask for students who are fans of mystery or suspense novels, movies, or TV shows to share the names of their favorite detectives or secret agents. If students need help, you may want to suggest some well-known sleuths and spies, such as Sir Arthur Conan Doyle's Sherlock Holmes, Agatha Christie's Inspector Poirot, secret agent James Bond, *Mission Impossible's* Ethan Hunt, Sydney Bristow from TV's *Alias*, or detectives Goren and Eames of *Law and Order: Criminal Intent*. Invite teenagers to describe their favorite scenes, stories, and episodes and see if they can identify specific traits of mystery writing that the various stories have in common.

Then say: **Today we're going to look closely at some clues about a hidden identity. And believe it or not, this "mystery" story is found in the Bible.**

EXPLORATION

Introduce the "crime" by inviting a student to read Isaiah 1:2-4. Ask:

- **What seems to be the problem in this passage?**

Once the students have sufficiently explored the idea of sin, guilt, faithlessness, and rebellion, have another student volunteer to read Isaiah 1:18. Then ask:

- **What does this passage say about the solution to the problem that we identified in Isaiah 1:2-4?**

Say: **At this point, the author has given us the problem and the solution. But what we don't have yet is *how* God is going to solve the problem.**

In some ways the book of Isaiah reads like a mystery novel. But rather than looking for a criminal, the author is leading us to discover a hero. Early on we find the first clue to the identity of this hero—a prophecy that God is going to give a sign to his people. The rest of the book contains more clues—who is God sending? How can we identify him? What is he like? And, for what purpose is the hero being sent?

Explain to the students that they are now going to get a chance to study the book of Isaiah, and encourage them to use their investigative skills.

Invite a student to read aloud Isaiah 7:13-17, the first clue to the mystery, while the rest of the teenagers read along.

Help them to launch into their investigation by asking:

> **LEADER TIP**
>
> It may be helpful to point out that the word *virgin* in this passage can also refer more generally to a young woman without children.

- **What clues or important details do we learn about the child from this passage?**

Encourage students to read carefully. If they need help, guide them to the clues: "a sign," "a virgin," "a son," "Immanuel," "eats curds and honey," "when he knows enough," and the presence of "Assyria."

Discuss with students that, like any good mystery plot, Isaiah then goes on to introduce some "leading suspects." These suspects may or may not match the identity of the secret hero. Launch teenagers quickly into their investigative groups by having the students form small groups of four to six and directing them to "Leading Suspects" (p. 6) in their Student Journals.

Challenge each group to come to a conclusion about both suspects presented in their Student Journals: Maher-Shalal-Hash-Baz and Hezekiah. Is either suspect the promised son that Isaiah speaks of? Give groups about 15 to 20 minutes to complete their discussion.

In their Student Journals, youth will read Isaiah 7:13-17 to discover clues about the coming hero, then will examine Isaiah 8:1-10 and consider if Maher-Shalal-Hash-Baz is a match. If students need help, point them to important repeated words and phrases that initially lead us to believe Maher-Shalal-Hash-Baz is the one: "son" in 8:3 (pointing back to 7:14), "knows how to say 'My father' or 'My mother' " in 8:4 (hints at "knows enough" in 7:15), and "Immanuel" along with "God is with us" in 8:8, 10 (refers us to 7:14).

Next in their journals, the students will read a second set of clues in 9:6-7. Students will go on to read Isaiah 36:1; 37:30-35; and 38:1-7 to determine if King Hezekiah fits both the first and second set of clues. You may need to assist students to connect some of the clues in this section.

- First, there are the words "sign" and "eat" in 37:30, which point us back to 7:14-15.
- Also, there is the presence of Assyria in 37:33 that brings to mind 7:17.
- Furthermore, Hezekiah's title as the king connects him with the royal language used in 9:6-7 (government, prince).
- There is the phrase "the zeal of the Lord" in 37:32 that is borrowed from 9:7.
- On top of all this, there is the name David that appears in both 37:35 and 9:7.

Encourage students to go back and forth between passages and questions to create a thorough list of clues and matching evidence. Finally, the Student Journals will lead them to discover a twist in this mystery. They will find a third set of clues, which will dismiss both leading suspects as more details are given away about the hero in 42:1-4; 49:5-7; 50:4-10; 52:13–53:12.

As youth gather back into a large group, say: **When people sit down to begin reading a mystery novel, the question they immediately** have is, "Who is the villain?" Now, as we begin to look at Isaiah, I want you to ask yourself, "Who is this hero of Isaiah's?" Like a mystery, the further along we get in Isaiah, the more details are revealed about the identity of this hero.

Ask students to shout out the conclusions of their discussion, helping you to create a linear chart showing the progression of Isaiah on a sheet of newsprint. Begin with the promised son in chapter 7, then the character of Maher-Shalal-Hash-Baz, the promised son in chapter 9, and so on. Draw a horizontal arrow, then add in the clues and events students shout out.

When the summary chart is done, ask:

• **What evidence leads you to believe that Maher-Shalal-Hash-Baz is *not* the promised son? Explain.**

• **What evidence leads you to believe that Hezekiah is *not* the promised son? Explain.**

Summarize the most important clues that the coming Immanuel would be a king and would also be a servant. For these reasons, neither Maher-Shalal-Hash-Baz nor Hezekiah meet the criteria, for Maher-Shalal-Hash-Baz is not a king, and Hezekiah is not a servant.

Say: **Just like us, early readers of Isaiah would have had these questions and ideas. They'd read about Maher-Shalal-Hash-Baz and wonder, "Is he the one?" Then they'd read about Hezekiah and think, "Maybe *he's* the one!" But Isaiah leaves us only with more clues...and the identity of the Messiah remains hidden.**

Ask, rhetorically: **Who is this promised son?**

Invite students to summarize the clues and traits they've discovered about the coming Messiah. Help them to include the idea that the hero would be born of a virgin, would be "God with us," and would be both a king (7:13-15; 9:6-7) and a servant (50:4-10).

LEADER TIP

Point out the Study 1 "On Your Own" section in the Student Journals on page 5, and encourage teenagers to use the personal Bible study and reflection suggestions in their devotional time during the week.

Say: **All these threads, plus many others throughout Isaiah, are woven together as a single tapestry, creating a great image of hope for the Jews in the Old Testament—a hope that was to come in the form of a single hero, who will be both servant and king, who...**(add descriptions that students mentioned).

TRANSFORMATION

Have students return to their small groups and discuss these questions. Ask:

- **How do you typically think of a king? What words, behaviors, or images come to mind?**
- **How do you typically think of a servant? What words, behaviors, or images come to mind?**
- **What do you think of the idea that the coming Messiah would be both a servant and a king? Do these two ideas fit together? Why or why not?**
- **How is the idea of a servant-king unique? How does it compare to leaders in the world today?**
- **If you were a Jewish person living during Old Testament times and were waiting for the coming Messiah, how would these prophecies encourage you?**
- **Why must the Messiah be both a king and a servant? Why must he both rule and suffer?**

Wrap up the study by inviting students to gather back together and share some of their insights from their discussion, making sure to summarize the main points of their Bible passage.

Then say: **Detectives look for clues by checking phone records, interviewing witnesses, or checking for fingerprints. As we've discovered, the book of Isaiah is *full* of clues about the promised son—clues that tell us what to look for, clues that will soon help us discover the real Messiah.**

Pass around the ink pad and the self-stick notes and invite students to put their thumb on the ink pad and then make a thumbprint on a self-stick note. When their ink has dried, encourage them to stick their "clue note" near the passage in Isaiah that contained a clue about the Messiah that meant the most to them during the Bible study.

LEADER TIP

In Study 12, you'll need to pass out a bunch of newspapers from a variety of dates, so start collecting them now.

Say: **In the final clue of Isaiah regarding the hero, the servant-king, we find these words: "The Spirit of the Sovereign Lord is on me, because the Lord has anointed me to preach good news to the poor. He has sent me to bind up the brokenhearted, to proclaim freedom for the captives and release from darkness for the prisoners, to proclaim the year of the Lord's favor"** (Isaiah 61:1-2a). **Although every clue discovered will be important in confirming the identity of the Messiah, these words from Isaiah 61 are those that the true Messiah will use to identify himself. In the coming weeks, we're going to discover the true identity of this Messiah, the Anointed One, the hero about whom Isaiah prophesied. And we are going to learn about the difference he can make in our own lives.**

Close by inviting students to spend a few moments in silent prayer, asking God to open their hearts in anticipation of the things he is going to teach them about the promised Messiah.

The Birth—O Holy Night!

Scripture Focus: Matthew 1:18-24; 2:1-12; Luke 1:26-38; 2:1-20; John 1:1-14

Supplies: Bibles; Student Journals; pens or pencils; baby pictures of students (see Preparation on this page); globe; 2 sheets of newsprint; marker; bag of rice (uncooked); bowl; antibacterial hand sanitizer gel (or sanitizing baby wipes); gift wrap; cardboard box; paper; TV (optional); VCR or DVD player (optional); *Jesus of Nazareth* video or DVD (optional); CD player (optional); Jewel's *Joy—A Holiday Collection* CD (optional); CD of reflective, worshipful music (optional)

> *"What one of us can understand a love so great that we would willingly limit our unlimitedness, put the flesh of mortality over our immortality, accept all the pain and grief of humanity, submit to betrayal by that humanity, be killed by it, and die a total failure (in human terms)…?"*
> —Madeleine L'Engle, ***The Irrational Season***

PREPARATION

Before the meeting, read the Leader Insight section to dive deeper into the topic of Jesus' birth. Then read through the study to familiarize yourself with the Scripture passages and activities.

For the **Connection** activity, you'll need to acquire baby pictures of some of the teenagers in your youth group. You'll need one picture for every four students at the meeting. It is very important that the picture was taken when the baby was one year old or younger, that the picture does *not* have a name printed anywhere on it, that other recognizable people (such as parents) aren't in the picture, and that

When an object moves through the Earth's atmosphere, the air molecules cause friction and the object heats up. These objects enter our atmosphere quietly and usually go unnoticed. A few people, however, sometimes catch a glimpse of these flashes that disrupt the peaceful sky.

Like debris breaking through into our atmosphere, the brilliant "meteor shower" of divine events recorded in the opening chapters of Matthew and Luke went unnoticed by many. Yet, when one steps back to look at history, one can see that the space and time that occupies the first century is riddled with divine activity, disrupting a period known as the *Pax Romana*, a peaceful time in the Mediterranean world extending from 27 B.C. to A.D. 180.

In this quiet period of history, an angel appears to Zechariah, foretelling the birth of John the Baptist. Then, an angel visits Mary and foretells Jesus' birth. John's birth soon follows, and quickly thereafter Jesus "breaks through" into our world. Several other significant events follow: Angels appear to nearby shepherds; Simeon is lead into the temple courts by the Spirit when Jesus is presented at the temple; and the Magi visit Jesus. History seems to converge on the birth of Jesus and its surrounding events, quietly announcing the arrival of the long-anticipated Messiah. Just as we "groan inwardly...for... the redemption of our bodies" (Romans 8:23), the Jewish people groaned for the arrival of this Anointed One.

But the "breaking through" is what makes the whole thing noteworthy. The flashes in the sky announce the divine becoming human. This is the exciting and life-changing bit of theology known to us as the incarnation. It is an essential tenet of the Christian faith and has been heavily guarded throughout history.

It didn't take long after the time of Christ for this idea to be attacked. By the second century, docetism had started to take root in Christianity. Docetism

the baby isn't easily recognizable. In other words, students shouldn't be able to look at the picture and immediately guess who it is.

Explain to those whose pictures you'll be using that their photograph will be part of a discussion activity and that they should not tell any of their friends that they've donated a picture. Let them know that part of the activity will involve other students guessing who the baby in the picture is, so you'd like them to keep their involvement strictly confidential.

purports that Jesus did not actually become human, but only appeared as if he did. The term *docetism* comes from the Greek word *dokeo*, "to seem or appear." This view of Jesus essentially denied that Jesus suffered, for God could not truly suffer.

In defense of the incarnation, some offered the concept of *logos* (Greek for "word") in response: The Word became *flesh* and made his *dwelling* among us (John 1:14, emphasis added). The "Word" here in John evokes Genesis 1:1, in which God's word is spoken at Creation. The connection is emphatically drawn by John's intentional use of "In the beginning," which is unmistakably taken from Genesis 1:1.

Whereas docetism made the heretical error of denying Jesus' humanity, *Arianism* made the opposite error: denying his deity. Early in the fourth century A.D., Arius claimed that Jesus was *not* actually God, but merely the son of God, the highest of all God's creation. In 325 the Council of Nicaea fired back with "We believe in one Lord, Jesus Christ, the only Son of God, eternally begotten of the Father, God from God, Light from Light, true God from true God, begotten, not made, of one being with the Father"—an adequate response that would eventually quell the Arian heresy.

Both views, docetism and Arianism, threatened the idea that Jesus was a sufficient sacrifice. The first claimed that he was not a real sacrifice; the second denied that he was a good-enough sacrifice. In other words, to balk at the incarnation of Jesus—seeing him as less than fully God and fully human—is to deny truth, and therefore to promote heresy. During this study, emphasize to students the central truth that Jesus was both fully God and fully man.

For the **Exploration** section, you'll need a globe. You'll also need to set up three study and worship stations in your meeting area, preferably in three corners of the room. (If you're able, you could set them up in three different rooms in your building.) For the first station, write the letter A on a paper and post it on the wall. Fill a bowl with uncooked rice and set it on the floor near the letter.

For the second station, post the letter B on the wall and set out a bottle of hand sanitizer gel—the type that evaporates after being rubbed onto your hands. (If you're unable to find hand sanitizer gel, use sanitizing wipes—like baby wipes—instead.)

For the last station, you'll need to wrap a cardboard box in gift wrap so it looks like a present. Cut a slit in the top (into which students can drop pieces of paper), and set it near the letter C that you'll post on the wall. You'll also need to cut small slips of paper and set them on the floor at this station; you'll need one slip of paper per student.

For the **Transformation** section, set up the TV and VCR or DVD player and cue up *Jesus of Nazareth*. Set the timer at 0:00:00 when the studio logo appears at the start of the movie, then fast-forward to approximately 0:47:00 with the image of the star over Bethlehem. In addition, plug in your CD player and prepare it to play "O Holy Night" on the *Joy—A Holiday Collection* CD. (There are several other great recordings of this song on other CDs, so if you have a different version, go ahead and use that.) If you don't have access to this movie or CD, that's OK. Just use the non-media suggestion for the concluding activity on page 28.)

Last, tape two sheets of newsprint to the wall.

CONNECTION

Welcome students to the Bible study, and start things off with a fun discussion. Have youth form teams of four and spread out around the room. Give each small group one of the baby pictures you acquired before the study. Don't tell students these are pictures of teenagers in your group—just tell them you collected some photos from some friends. (Also, be sure not to give a picture of a student to the group that student is actually in.)

> **LEADER TIP**
>
> If your group has fewer than 12 students, have teenagers form small groups of only 2 or 3.

Prompt small groups to look at their picture and try to come to a conclusion about the child's personality and other traits based on the photograph. Groups should discuss these questions:

- **What can you tell about this kid from this picture—gender, approximate age, and so on?**
- **What would you guess are the child's personality traits?**

- **If you had to make a prediction, what do you think this baby will be like when he or she gets older—personality, talents, hobbies, and so on?**

After 5 to 10 minutes or when small groups have wrapped up their discussion, explain that each of these baby pictures is a photograph of a teenager in the youth group. Allow each small group one guess regarding the identity of the baby—if they don't get it right on their first try, go ahead and reveal the true identity.

Have small groups discuss:

- **How did your guesses about the baby's traits and future personality compare to the actual person?**

Gather everyone back together and say: **Today we're going to study God's coming to earth and being born as a human baby. We're going to look more closely at what the circumstances of Jesus' birth teach us about his traits, personality, and purpose on earth.**

EXPLORATION

Place the globe before the group and say: **When an object moves through the Earth's atmosphere, the air molecules cause friction and the object heats up. (This is why a space shuttle has a heat shield.) These objects enter our atmosphere quietly and usually go unnoticed. A few people, however, sometimes catch a glimpse of the streak in the sky.**

A famous hymn includes this line: "Long lay the world in sin and error pining, till he appeared and the soul felt its worth." Among the common and quiet lives of those living in the first century, many events announced the arrival of the Christ. God had entered this world in the womb of a humble Jewish girl. (Turn the globe and point to the general area of Nazareth, modern-day Israel). **For the majority of people, this event went unnoticed. But for a few, this event captured their attention and demanded their whole being. Today we're going to take notice of this event and learn about a baby boy, his traits, personality, and purpose on earth.** Ask:

- **What do you know about Jesus' birth?**

Invite students to brainstorm all the basic facts they already know, such as his miraculous conception, his birth in a manger in Bethlehem, his visit by shepherds, and so on. Write the students' answers on a sheet of newsprint, attempting to list them in basic chronological order. If students overlook any significant events, jog their memories by asking:

• **What else? Any other details?**

Make sure all of the important details are included in your list, and add some yourself if needed.

Then say: **John, Jesus' beloved disciple, knew all of these details—yet he chose to write about Jesus' birth in a totally different way.**

Have students return to their foursomes and read together John 1:1-14. Prompt them to discuss these questions by asking one question at a time and allowing students to discuss it before moving on to the next question. Allow about two to three minutes for each discussion question.

• **What words or phrases stand out to you? Why?**

• **Why do you think John chose to use poetic language?**

• **What traits or characteristics of Jesus do we learn about from John?**

Prompt small groups to read the definition of *incarnation* in their

> For your convenience, here's what the Student Journal says about the term *incarnation:*
>
> The word *incarnation* comes from the Latin words *in carne,* which literally mean "in flesh." God, the creator of the universe—the powerful, eternal, loving, ultimate Being—took on human flesh. Because of his love for humanity, he came to earth in the person of Jesus. As the *New Bible Dictionary* explains, "God, without ceasing to be God, was made man...When the Word 'became flesh' his deity was not abandoned, or reduced, or contracted." In other words, Jesus, in a mysterious and divine way that is difficult to comprehend, was both fully God and fully human. He was God...with skin on.

Student Journals on page 10. Ask:

- **Which verses or phrases in John 1:1-14 best describe the idea of the incarnation?**
- **How would you describe the idea of the incarnation in your own words?**
- **What is most amazing to you about God becoming human?**

Have small groups read Eugene Peterson's rendition of John 1:14 from *The Message* on page 10 of their Student Journals. Ask:

- **How does this version of John 1:14 add to your understanding of the incarnation?**

After students have discussed the question, say: **Let's look more closely at what actually happened when God "moved into the neighborhood."**

> For your convenience, here is the text of John 1:14 from *The Message:*
>
> "The Word became flesh and blood,
> and moved into the neighborhood.
> We saw the glory with our own eyes,
> the one-of-a-kind glory,
> like Father, like Son,
> Generous inside and out,
> true from start to finish." —John 1:14

Explain that you'd like teenagers to choose a partner from their foursome. They'll have about 20 minutes to journey together to three different study and worship stations set up in your room. They should take their Bibles, Student Journals, and pens or pencils with them to each station. Direct them to turn to pages 11-13 in their Student Journals where they'll find instructions.

At each station they'll be prompted to read a Bible passage, discuss it with their partner, and creatively respond to the passage in some way.

Each study and worship station focuses on a certain aspect of Jesus' birth; students may go to the stations in any order they'd like, as long as they're sure to visit each station and follow the instructions. Direct students to turn to page 14 in their Student Journals where they'll find space to write notes from each station. Point out the location of each station and have students get started. If you're able, play soft worshipful or meditative music in the background while students study and pray.

For your convenience, here's a basic summary of what students will do at each station.

Station A

Youth will study the Annunciation and Mary's pregnancy in Matthew 1:18-24 and Luke 1:26-38. They'll learn basics about prenatal development and will hold a piece of rice that is the approximate size of a 30-day-old fetus. Pairs will discuss the mystery of the incarnation.

Station B

Students will compare the circumstances of Jesus' birth in Luke 2:1-7 with those of a standard hospital birth in a first-world country today. They'll use hand sanitizer as an object lesson and will consider what the humble circumstances of Jesus' birth teach about his traits and his purpose.

Station C

Teenagers will study Luke 2:8-20 and Matthew 2:1-12 to learn about Jesus' two sets of visitors: the shepherds and the Magi. They'll discuss and write down a specific personal commitment to honor Jesus and will put it in a gift box.

After students have visited every station, gather the group back together and invite students to share highlights of their Student Journal notes answering the question "What do you learn about Jesus?" from the various Scripture passages and station activities. Encourage students as they share, and ask them follow-up questions such as, "What does this tell us about Jesus' purpose?" "Why is that significant?" or "What does that mean to you personally?"

Summarize the key points from teenagers' ideas, then say: **As we**

LEADER TIP

If some students finish all the stations early, invite them to sit in an area that won't distract the rest of the teenagers who are visiting the stations. Ask them to quietly read through their notes and write down additional thoughts or questions.

discussed earlier, Jesus was fully God and fully human.

Draw a vertical line down the center of a second sheet of newsprint, creating two columns. Write "Amazing" at the top of one column and "Common" at the top of the other column. Ask:

• **What was amazing about Jesus' birth and points to his deity?** Write students' ideas in the "Amazing" column. Students might say things like: "His mother was a virgin, so her pregnancy was a miracle" or "Angels dramatically announced his birth."

Then ask:

• **What was common or plain about Jesus' birth and points to his humanity?** and write their answers in the "Common" column. Youth might have ideas like: "His parents were just normal people" or "He was born in a stable."

After students have exhausted their ideas, add observations of your own to the columns. Then say: **The events and circumstances surrounding Jesus' birth and infancy point to the amazing truth of the incarnation. Just as Jesus was both fully God and fully human, the events that surrounded his birth were both totally amazing and starkly common. The amazing and all-powerful God who created the entire universe entered his creation and was born as an infant because of his love for us.**

LEADER TIP

Point out the Study 2 "On Your Own" section in the Student Journals on page 9, and encourage teenagers to use the personal Bible study and reflection suggestions in their devotional time during the week.

TRANSFORMATION

Wrap things up with a time of worship. Explain that as students watch a video and listen to a song, you'd like them to quietly reflect on the amazing mystery of the incarnation demonstrated in Jesus' birth. Play the *Jesus of Nazareth* video clip you prepared, beginning at approximately 0:47:00 when the scene focuses on the star over Bethlehem. Play the clip with the sound muted as you simultaneously play the song "O Holy Night" sung by Jewel on the CD *Joy—A Holiday Collection*. Invite students to read along with the song—the lyrics are printed on page 15 of their Student Journal and are also included below for your own personal meditation. Stop the clip when the song is done.

NON-MEDIA OPTION

If you aren't able to play the video or listen to the "O Holy Night" recording, instead ask students to silently read through all the lyrics of the song (page 15 of the Student Journal) and then read (or sing) "O Holy Night" together as a concluding prayer.

O Holy Night
by Placide Cappeau

O holy night, the stars are brightly shining;

It is the night of the dear Savior's birth!

Long lay the world in sin and error pining,

Till He appeared and the soul felt its worth.

A thrill of hope, the weary soul rejoices,

For yonder breaks a new and glorious morn.

Fall on your knees, O hear the angel voices!

O night divine, O night when Christ was born!

O night, O holy night, O night divine!

Study 3

The Baptism—the Son of God

Scripture Focus: Matthew 3:1-17; Mark 1:1-8; Luke 1:5-25, 39-45, 57-80; 3:1-20; John 1:29-42
Supplies: Bibles; Student Journals; pens or pencils; *Unbreakable* video or DVD (optional); TV (optional); VCR or DVD player (optional); several Bible study tools such as commentaries on the Gospels, Bible dictionaries, study Bibles, and concordances; large sheet of newsprint; markers; tape or pins; *O Brother, Where Art Thou?* CD (optional); CD player (optional)

> *"In his baptism Jesus identified with sinners, something which even John the Baptist found scandalous (Mt. 3:14). It was an anticipation of Calvary, when his cross was to be his baptism—in blood…The baptism of Jesus was an assurance of sonship…[and] it was a commissioning for costly service."*
> —Michael Green, **The Complete Book of Everyday Christianity**

PREPARATION

Before the meeting, read the Leader Insight section to dive deeper into the topic of Jesus' baptism. Then read through the study to familiarize yourself with the Scripture passages and activities.

For the **Connection** activity, you'll need a TV, a VCR or DVD player, and a video or DVD of the film *Unbreakable*. Cue up the film by setting the timer at 0:00:00 when the studio logo appears at the start of the film. Fast-forward to approximately 0:44:45 with a close-up of David Dunn (Bruce Willis) lifting weights. If you're not able to use this movie clip, instead find a comic book to use to launch your discussion.

In the Old Testament, washing in water was an essential aspect of ritual cleansing and was a necessary and regular practice for God-fearing Jews when holy matters were involved. In Leviticus 16:4 a priest is commanded to bathe in water before putting on the sacred garments and entering the sanctuary on the Day of Atonement. Also, a person healed of a skin disease is required to wash in water (Leviticus 14:8-9), as is a person who comes into contact with a corpse (Numbers 19:12). In all three cases the washing in water results in cleanliness.

A few Old Testament passages go one step further: Jeremiah 4:14; Ezekiel 36:25; and Zechariah 13:1 speak not only of washing as a means of cleansing, but more specifically of a washing and cleansing from sin. When one finally reaches John baptizing in the Gospel accounts, he is preaching, "Repent, for the kingdom of heaven is near." Repentance from what? It seems likely that John is connecting with the Old Testament concept of cleansing, and he is building on the references to water as a sign of cleansing from sin. However, John seems to add new emphasis to the idea of cleansing in water as a sign of *repentance* from sin.

It is not difficult then to sympathize with John's question when Jesus asks him for his baptism of repentance: "I need to be baptized by you, and do you come to me?" (Matthew 3:14). After all, of what sin could Jesus possibly repent?

Though still insisting to be baptized, Jesus responds, "It is proper for us to do this to fulfill all righteousness." What does this mean? Why did Jesus ask to be baptized if not for sin?

Some answer this question by saying that Jesus was identifying with sinners who are in need of repentance. Though this element of Jesus' baptism should not be missed, perhaps his words should be understood in a larger sense, going beyond the event of the baptism. When looking at the span of

For the **Exploration** section, you'll need multiple Bible study tools such as concordances, Bible dictionaries, study Bibles, and commentaries on the Gospels. You'll need at least one study tool for every four students in your group. Also, cut a sheet of newsprint about 6 feet long.

If you're using the optional CD in the **Transformation** section, plug in the CD player and prepare to play the song "Down to the River to Pray" on the *O Brother, Where Art Thou?* CD.

Jesus' life on earth, it is perhaps best to view the primary significance of his baptism as being the events surrounding the actual baptism: John's declaration, "Look, the Lamb of God" (John 1:29); Jesus' anointing by the Spirit; and John's announcement, "This is the Son of God" (John 1:34). This is the first event in which Jesus is revealed to the public as the Messiah. It serves as a marker for the beginning of Jesus' ministry. After this point, all other events in Jesus' life move toward his death and resurrection. John's baptism of Jesus set into motion the events that culminated on the cross and in the tomb, bringing salvation to the world, hence, "to fulfill all righteousness."

Immediately after Jesus is baptized, two events unmistakably reveal Jesus as the Messiah. First, after Jesus comes up out of the water, a voice from heaven declares, "This is my Son, whom I love; with him I am well pleased" (Matthew 3:17). This statement brings to mind Psalm 2:7: "You are my Son; today I have become your Father." Second, the observers witness the dove-like appearance of the Spirit descending on Jesus. For a Jewish audience, this would recall the book of Isaiah: In Isaiah 11:1-2, the prophet writes, "A shoot will come up from the stump of Jesse...The Spirit of the Lord will rest on him." When speaking of the servant in 42:1, the book of Isaiah reads, "I will put my Spirit on him."

In three of the four Gospel accounts, the baptism of Jesus is closely followed by the calling of the disciples. However, in the Gospel of Luke a brief incident interrupts this flow. In Luke 4:18 Jesus walks into a Nazarene synagogue, receives the scroll of Isaiah, and reads from 61:1, "The Spirit of the Lord is on me..." He continues, "Today this scripture is fulfilled in your hearing." Although this point will come up in Study 7, "The Stone or the Cross?" you might find it relevant to make the connection for your students between the baptism of Jesus and Jesus' own declaration to be *the* anointed one in Luke 4.

CONNECTION

Greet teenagers and begin by showing them a short clip from the film *Unbreakable*. The scene starts at approximately 0:44:45 with a close-up of David Dunn (Bruce Willis) lifting weights as his son looks on. Play the clip until approximately 0:49:55 when Dunn answers his son's question, "How much is it, Dad?" by saying, "About 350 pounds." Explain before playing it that in this clip the son's suspicions of his dad being a real-life superhero are confirmed.

After the movie clip ask:

- **What would you do if you discovered that someone close to you—like your parent—was a superhero?**
- **How would that change your relationship?**
- **Would this realization change you personally? If so, how?**
- **What if you realized a person was God in the flesh? How would you recognize him?**
- **How would this affect you?**

NON-MEDIA OPTION

If you aren't able to play the scene from *Unbreakable*, instead have everybody gather together. If you can, acquire a superhero comic book and show it to the students. Whether you have this or not, ask:

- Who are your favorite comic book superheroes?
- What would you do if you discovered that someone close to you—like your parent—was a superhero?
- How would that change your relationship?
- Would this realization change you personally? If so, how?
- What if you realized a person was God in the flesh? How would you recognize him?
- How would this affect you?

EXPLORATION

Invite a volunteer to read aloud John 1:29-34, then ask:

- **If you had never heard of John the Baptist or Jesus, and you were standing by and heard this testimony of John's, what would you understand it to mean?**
- **What questions would you have had?**
- **What would you have likely thought about John's statement that Jesus was the Son of God?**
- **What would you guess had happened prior to this time that would prompt John to make such a claim about another man?**

Say: **John's conclusion about Jesus was radical. He claimed— before others—that this was no ordinary man! This Jesus was the Son of God! Why would John make such a claim?**

Divide students into groups of four in which they'll examine the life of John the Baptist and learn more about the events that led up to John's dramatic conclusion about Jesus. Assign half of the groups to study the infancy and childhood of John the Baptist and the other group to study the adult years of John the Baptist.

Direct students to page 18 in their Student Journals and clarify that the groups examining the start of John's life should use Luke 1:5-25, 39-45, and 57-80 as their primary texts. Those studying John's adult years should focus on Matthew 3:1-12; Luke 3:1-20; and Mark 1:1-8. (Prompt students to write their group's Scripture references in the "Key Scriptures" blank in their Student Journal.)

> ## LEADER TIP
>
> If you have fewer than eight students, just divide your group in half for this activity. These study groups can be as small as two people.

Set out the Bible study tools in the middle of the room and explain that you'd like small groups to follow the instructions in their Student Journal as they independently research the life of John the Baptist. Encourage them to use several different Bible study tools so their research has greater depth and insight. Let students know that they'll have about 20 minutes to research before they're called back to the group to report what they've learned.

Give students a three-minute warning so they can wrap up their research. When 20 minutes have passed, call everyone back together.

Lay out the newsprint banner and ask a male volunteer to lay on it so the group can draw the silhouette of a human body. The person can lay in any pose he wants—just make sure that one arm is either straight out, is pointing up, or is at his side and bent at the elbow pointing out. He should be pointing with the index finger on that hand, and that arm and hand should be visible in the silhouette.

Give students markers so they can trace the silhouette, then hang up the silhouette with tape or pins. Invite small groups to take turns presenting their findings, using markers to turn the silhouette into a representation of John the Baptist. Explain that small groups should write words or short phrases that describe events or circumstances *outside* of the silhouette. Words or phrases that describe John's character or personality can be written *inside* the silhouette.

Groups may also draw on "John" any important physical traits (such as camel-hair clothes, the eating of a bug, and so on). When groups make their presentations, ask each group to share one interesting thing that they learned from using a study tool, such as another Bible verse (outside of their assigned reading), a quote from a commentary, or a thought-provoking explanation from a Bible dictionary.

Limit groups to sharing just two or three traits of John and one interesting thing from a study tool, then move to the next group.

LEADER TIP

If you only have one study tool per group, call out "Switch" every few minutes so that groups pass their study tool to the next group. This will allow students to be exposed to a variety of Bible study tools. If youth aren't familiar with how to use the study tools, take a few minutes to explain how to use each particular tool.

Continue rotating from group to group until each team has shared all of its relevant ideas. (This method of presentation will prevent a scenario in which one team shares all the interesting information about John, leaving another group without anything to share.)

When everyone is done presenting their study results, congratulate them on their research efforts and repeat some of the key traits or facts listed on the John silhouette. Also compliment students on any particularly artful or humorous drawings on John.

Say: **Now that we know a lot more about who this guy John really was, let's reexamine the incredible claim he publicly made about Jesus.**

Ask a volunteer to read aloud John 1:29-34 while everyone else reads along in their Bibles.

Refer teenagers to the portrait of John they created, then ask:

• **How would these traits and events prepare John to make his declaration about Jesus? Explain.**

• **What are John's "credentials" that make his declaration authoritative?**

Say: **The other Gospel writers describe in greater detail the event John refers to in verse 32.**

Invite another volunteer to read aloud Matthew 3:13-17.

Instruct students to close their eyes and imagine that they were present during Jesus' baptism. Read the following to them slowly and dramatically: **Imagine you were there that day. Step into the sandals of one of the members of the crowd.**

Jesus always seemed to be followed by crowds—people coming to be baptized, people coming to hear him speak, people coming to find answers to their spiritual questions.

You're sitting near the banks of the Jordan River. Imagine the hot sun beating down. Imagine the sound of the water, lapping along the banks of the river. Imagine the sounds of others chatting, talking, or perhaps praying. Imagine seeing people wade into the cool water to be baptized by John.

Then someone new shows up. He wades out into the water. He speaks to John, and it sounds like John is arguing with him. The man says something—it's hard to hear. Then John nods his head and baptizes the man, dunking him under the water.

As soon as the man is brought back up out of the water, the sky shines brightly, blindingly. You gasp and try to catch your breath. You rub your eyes in disbelief. A form—a spirit—looking almost like a dove—hovers down from the sky.

Suddenly a sound—a voice unlike any you've heard before—calls out from nowhere—from *everywhere*—saying, "This is my Son, whom I love; with him I am well pleased."

Then the light fades; everything is back to normal.

LEADER TIP

This method of using imagination to spiritually "relocate" oneself to the scene of a biblical event is deeply rooted in Christian history. Ignatius of Loyola wrote about this type of prayer in his *Spiritual Exercises,* calling it "contemplation," with its sense of "being there and looking"—experiencing, hearing, tasting, and smelling—rather than just logically thinking about scriptural accounts. Consider using this imaginative reading and prayer approach in other aspects of your youth ministry.

John is in the water with the man. You stare at them in awe.

When you're done, ask students to share with a partner one thought or question they would have had if they were there in the crowd the day Jesus was baptized. Also ask them to talk about what they would've done next after seeing this happen.

TRANSFORMATION

Say: **Let's look at how some followers of John *did* respond.**

Prompt pairs to read John 1:35-42 to see what happened next.

Ask the group:

- **What do you think motivated Andrew and the other man to spend a day with Jesus?**
- **What might have caused them to declare Jesus was the Messiah?**

Refer back to the students' silhouette of John the Baptist and write the word "Jesus" near the pointing index finger. Ask:

- **How did John the Baptist effectively point others to Jesus?**

Wrap things up by directing youth to page 19 in their Student Journals. Encourage them to follow the instructions there for a time of personal prayer and reflection.

If you're able, play the song "Down to the River to Pray" from the *O Brother, Where Art Thou?* CD during this personal prayer and writing time. This song is a traditional folk song about baptism and one's commitment to God.

When they're done writing, lead the group in a concluding prayer, praying something like this: **Lord, thank you for the example you set for us in baptism. Thank you for the inspiring life of John the Baptist. Help us, Lord, to point others to you as John the Baptist did. Help us to be like Andrew and spend time getting to know you better. We love you, Jesus. Amen.**

LEADER TIP

Point out the Study 3 "On Your Own" section in the Student Journals on page 17, and encourage teenagers to use the personal Bible study and reflection suggestions in their devotional time during the week.

The Disciples—the Cost of Following

Scripture Focus: Matthew 4:18-25; Luke 6:12-16; 8:1-3; 14:25-33; John 8:12
Supplies: Bibles; Student Journals; pens or pencils; 1 photocopy of "And the Crowd Goes Wild!" handout (p. 43), cut apart; pillar or taper candle; candle stand or plate; 2 books of matches; metal pie tin; *No Name Face* CD by Lifehouse (optional); CD player (optional); 1 photocopy of "Risking It All" handout (pp. 44-45), cut apart; Bebo Norman's *Myself When I Am Real* CD (optional)

> *"I know Jesus' followers often enlist with high aspirations and expectations. Disciples step in line with unspoken yet heartfelt agendas…**I know where Jesus will take me**, the young disciples claim, and so they, like the first five [disciples], follow. And they, like the first five, are surprised."*
> —Max Lucado, **When God Whispers Your Name**

PREPARATION

Before the meeting, read the Leader Insight section to dive deeper into the topic of Jesus' followers. Then read through the study to familiarize yourself with the Scripture passages and activities.

For the **Connection** activity, you'll need to make one photocopy of the "And the Crowd Goes Wild!" handout (p. 43) and cut it into four sections.

For the **Exploration** section, you'll need to gather a pillar candle (or a taper candle), a candleholder, a metal pie tin, and two books of matches. You'll also need to make one copy of the "Risking It All" handout (pp. 44-45) and cut it into strips as indicated. Get the CD player ready to play Lifehouse's "Hanging by a Moment" from the CD *No Name Face*.

A passage youth will examine in this study that often raises questions is Jesus' statement in Luke 14:26. "If anyone comes to me and does not *hate* his father and mother, his wife and children, his brothers and sisters...he cannot be my disciple" (emphasis added). Students might be confused or concerned about Jesus' directive that his followers should hate their families. However, Jesus does not intend for his words to be taken literally; *hate* is used as hyperbole. Jesus often used hyperbole (see another example in Matthew 5:29-30). In contrasting hating one's family with being his disciple, Jesus adds force to his statement.

Another example of hyperbole is found in Romans 9:13 (Malachi 1:2-3): "Jacob I loved, but Esau I hated." Certainly God did not literally *hate* Esau, in the sense that we think of hate, but the hyperbole illustrates that his regard for Esau, in comparison to his love for Jacob, was *like* hate. Likewise, the contrast of hating one's family and following Christ is a device used to demonstrate that next to the immense and total love Jesus expected that we have for God, our love for our families is dwarfed in comparison.

In this study you'll also explore Jesus' comments in John 8:12. In this profound statement, Jesus calls himself the "light of the world" and promises that those who follow him "will never walk in darkness." What exactly is he

CONNECTION

Warmly welcome everyone as they arrive, then start things off by sharing some funny and bizarre true news stories. Ask for four volunteers and give each volunteer one of the stories from "And the Crowd Goes Wild!" handout (p. 43). Have volunteers take turns reading their stories aloud. Then ask:

- **Which of these stories was the funniest or most bizarre? Why?**

- **Which of these groups of fans seemed the most devoted? Why?**

- **What are some other funny or bizarre things you know of that people have done because they're followers of a person or group?**

Say: **Phish, the Bulls, Andrew Jackson, and Jessica Simpson may have had devoted followers, but none of them compare to the followers of Jesus. We're going to learn more about Jesus' followers and what it means to be a follower of Jesus today.**

saying? In this case some historical context will help extract the full impact of Jesus' claim. In the Jewish calendar, the people celebrate three major festivals. The first is the Feast of Unleavened Bread (Passover). The second is the Feast of Weeks. The final and most popular is the Feast of Tabernacles, which came at the conclusion of the harvest season in the fall, commemorating God's provision.

Beginning in John 7:10, Jesus attended the week-long Feast of Tabernacles in Jerusalem. In John 7:14, halfway through the festival, Jesus began to teach. It seems natural then to take 8:12 as a continuation of this teaching at the Feast.

With this in mind, Craig L. Blomberg makes the following observation in *The Historical Reliability of John's Gospel*: "Every night of the feast, four huge lamps were lit to accompany joyful singing and dancing. On the last night the main candelabrum was deliberately left unlit as a reminder that Israel had not yet experienced full salvation." The implications of this, Blomberg concludes, is that Jesus "declares himself to be that salvation, 'the light of the world.'" Again we see Jesus claiming to be the promised Messiah, the Savior of Israel. But now we see that his salvation is extended to those who follow him, for Jesus is the source of true life. As John states in his prologue, "In him was life, and that life was the light of men" (John 1:4).

EXPLORATION

Invite three volunteers to read aloud Matthew 4:18-25; Luke 8:1-3; and Luke 6:12-16.

Then say: **Huge crowds followed Jesus! Men and women dedicated their lives to him; gave him money, food, and shelter; hung on every word he said; and became some of his closest friends. Yet, though there were many men and women who followed Jesus and were totally devoted to him, today we're going to focus specifically on just 12 of them: the disciples.**

Have students sit in a circle on the floor, then prompt a student to read aloud John 8:12. Set the candle on the metal pie tin in the center of the circle and light it.

Then say: **Jesus was the light of the world. He promised his followers that they would never walk in darkness.**

Direct students to turn to pages 22-23 in their Student Journals.

Instruct them to quietly reflect on the "Light of the World" text in the Student Journal as they look at the candle. (The "Light of the World" text lists all of the disciples and prompts students to consider what it would have been like to be one of them.)

After a few minutes of reading and personal meditation, dim the lights in the room so students can focus just on the light of the candle. Grab the books of matches. Sit near the candle and use its light to read aloud Luke 14:33. Then distribute the 12 slips from the "Risking It All" handout to 12 students. If you have fewer than 12 students, distribute all the slips among the students you have.

Say: **We don't know with absolute certainty what happened to all of the disciples, but ancient church history passed down these accounts of their lives and deaths, which we'll explore now.**

One at a time and in numerical order, invite a teenage reader to come near to the candle. Have each volunteer read aloud the text on his or her slip describing the martyrdom or torture of one of the disciples then light a match using the flame on the candle.

The student should wait a second or so for everyone to see the flame, then should blow it out and drop it onto the metal pie tin. The lighted match represents the flame of each disciple's life; extinguishing the flame represents each disciple's death for the sake of Christ.

 ••••••Play the song "Hanging by a Moment" on Lifehouse's *No Name Face* CD. Before you hit "Play," say: **Listen to the words of this song as if you were one of the disciples.**

After the song, turn the lights back up and ask:

• **What words or phrases stood out to you? Why?**

• **How do these lyrics take on a new meaning when you listen to them from the perspective of the disciples?**

Have students form groups of three or four to discuss these questions. Ask:

- Which one of the disciples' deaths stands out to you the most? Why?
- What motivated the disciples to go through such pain for the sake of Jesus?
- In John 8:12, Jesus said his followers would never walk in darkness—yet dying in these brutal ways seems pretty dark. Were the disciples "tricked"? Explain.
- What do you think Jesus truly meant when he said "never walk in darkness"?

Have small groups read together Luke 14:25-33 and discuss the following questions:

- What simple observations can you make about being a disciple of Jesus from this paragraph?
- Does Jesus really want his followers to "hate" their families? What point is he trying to make?
- Jesus said this to the disciples *before* he was crucified, so they didn't necessarily have the same understanding of the phrase "carry his cross" (in Luke 14:27) that we have. If you were there, what would you have understood Jesus to be saying?
- What extra meaning does this phrase take on since we know that Jesus died for us on the cross?
- Jesus gives two examples of the importance of considering the cost of something before making a commitment to it. What are the "costs" of being a Christian today?
- What does it look like to be a fully committed disciple of Jesus?
- What challenges confront a person who takes Luke 14:33 seriously? Why is facing such challenges so hard to do?

Direct groups to wrap up their discussion by praying together about their own commitments to take up their crosses and that they will have the courage to live as fully committed followers of Jesus.

TRANSFORMATION

Have everybody gather back together as a large group to wrap things up and ask:

> • **Do Christians today take on the same risks the disciples did? Explain.**

Say: **If persecution, torture, and even death are what comes with being a disciple of Jesus, then who in the world would want to be one? What is it that motivates a person to truly consider the cost—to recognize the risks and challenges of being 100 percent committed to Jesus—and then step forward in faith? Being totally convinced of who Christ is will determine _your_ answer to the question. In our upcoming meetings, we'll watch as the disciples become convinced about who Jesus really is.**

We all must ask ourselves: What does it really mean to be a follower of Jesus? Though we may not face the same type of persecution the disciples endured, we must ask ourselves this: Are we willing to follow Jesus _no matter what?_

Allow students a minute to quietly ponder your challenge, then lead the group in a final prayer. You may want to pray something like this: **God, we are so inspired by the examples of your followers and what they were willing to endure in their determination to follow you. Help us to consider the cost of what it means to truly follow you. Help us reach a point of dedication where we're willing to risk everything because of our love for you. Help us know you more as we seek to be totally committed followers. Amen.**

LEADER TIP

You may want to play the song "Great Light of the World" from Bebo Norman's CD _Myself When I Am Real_ as a closing prayer. Ask students to consider how this song relates to the experience of the disciples and how it relates to their personal experience of faith.

LEADER TIP

Point out the Study 4 "On Your Own" section in the Student Journals on page 21, and encourage teenagers to use the personal Bible study and reflection suggestions in their devotional time during the week.

And the Crowd Goes Wild!

Instructions: Photocopy this page and cut apart these four true news stories. Give each to a student volunteer to read aloud to the group.

• •

The Manly Matadors

The Matadors are likely the most devoted Chicago Bulls fans ever. This "dance team" of 14 men, trained by professional choreographers, performs during Bulls basketball games. These overweight performers wear wigs and bare midriffs or go topless during their choreographed dances and chants—jiggling, belly-bouncing, and performing cheerleader-like moves to songs like "YMCA" and "Maniac"—and the crowds go wild.

• •

Phish Heads

When the band Phish played its last concert in 2004, about 65,000 "Phish heads" braved terrible weather to see the concert held in rural Vermont. Most had traveled from around the country to get to the small farming community. Due to roadblocks, about 6,000 fans had to walk miles in rain, fog, and mud to get to the show. Some fans paid over $900 per ticket.

• •

President Hides From Fans

When Andrew Jackson was inaugurated, he had to flee from his fans. A mob of 20,000 Jackson devotees celebrated like crazy, trashing the White House in the process. To lure the mobs out of the White House, presidential aides put bathtubs on the lawn and filled them with juice and whiskey to appeal to the drunken crowds. Things were so out of control that the president himself had to hide in a nearby hotel.

• •

Wal-Mart Brouhaha

When Jessica Simpson readied to sign autographs at a Wal-Mart store in Massachusetts, she didn't know what she was getting herself into. They expected about 500 fans. Instead, over 5,000 fans arrived, causing traffic jams, mobbing Simpson's limo, and massing around store entrances. The police had to shut down highways and escort Simpson out of the store because of the chaos. Several teenage fans were arrested, one of whom scratched a police officer's face in her desperate effort to see Simpson.

• •

Risking It All

1. James son of Zebedee was sentenced to death for his Christian faith. He was beheaded in A.D 44. (*Acts 12:2*)

2. In A.D. 54, **Philip** was whipped and then crucified because of his commitment to Jesus. (*according to Christian tradition*)

3. Matthew journeyed to Ethiopia to share his Christian faith. In A.D. 60, he was killed with a halberd—a weapon of a combined spear and ax. (*according to Christian tradition*)

4. James son of Alphaeus was beaten, stoned, and clubbed to death because of his devotion to Christ. (*according to Christian tradition*)

5. Matthias, the disciple who replaced Judas Iscariot, was stoned and then decapitated. (*according to Christian tradition*)

6. Andrew traveled to Asia to tell people about Jesus. It cost him his life—he was crucified on a cross that was stuck into the ground in an X shape. (*according to Christian tradition*)

7. Simon Peter was crucified because of his bold faith. He felt he wasn't worthy to be killed in the same way as Jesus, so he requested that he be crucified upside down. (*according to Christian tradition*)

8. In A.D. 72, Thaddaeus, also called **Jude**, like many of the other disciples, was crucified due to his faith. (*according to Christian tradition*)

9. Bartholomew went to many countries to tell others about Jesus. In the end, he was beaten and then crucified. (*according to Christian tradition*)

10. Thomas traveled to India to preach the gospel. Pagan priests had him impaled by a spear. (*according to Christian tradition*)

11. Simon the Zealot traveled abroad to tell others the good news. While preaching in Britain in A.D. 74, he was crucified. (*according to Christian tradition*)

12. John was thrown in a pot of boiling oil, then was banished to an isolated island. He was the only disciple who was not murdered for his faith. (*according to Christian tradition*)

The Power—the Miracles of Jesus

Scripture Focus: Mark 4:35-41; 5:1-43; 6:30-51
Supplies: Bibles; Student Journals; pens or pencils; paper; 1 nature object per student such as leaves, blades of grass, acorns, wildflowers, seeds, or twigs; a bucket; a few rolls of aluminum foil; tape; glue or glue sticks; a large piece of poster board or cardboard; several pairs of scissors; colored markers; other art supplies such as yarn, glitter, watercolors, magazines, and so on (optional); CD of worship music (optional); CD player (optional)

> "Although [the disciples] were in a great storm, **the power that made the storm was the very power to which they had to trust.** There was not a single blast of the tempest but Jehovah's might had sent it, nor did a single wave leap up, in apparent wrath, but with God's permission." —Charles Haddon Spurgeon, **The CH Spurgeon Collection, Volume 3: Miracles**

PREPARATION

Before the meeting, read the Leader Insight section to dive deeper into the topic of Jesus' power. Then read through the study to familiarize yourself with the Scripture passages and activities.

For the **Connection** activity, cut paper into small slips—about eight per sheet—enough for each student to have one.

For the **Transformation** activity, you'll need to collect a variety of lightweight objects from nature such as leaves, blades of grass, acorns, wildflowers, seeds, or twigs. You'll need one object per student. (If you're doing this study in winter and don't have many options for nature objects, use twigs and buy some sunflower seeds at

LEADER INSIGHT

The synoptic Gospels (Matthew, Mark, and Luke) are occasionally criticized for not perfectly matching up chronologically. But this is like criticizing a baker for not making meatloaf when the baker planned to present an assorted spread of cookies. Although the baker is a cook, and meatloaf is certainly food, it doesn't necessarily follow that the baker's concern is meatloaf. Likewise, a person does not pick up a history book expecting to get a novel, and one does not ask that a biography be a poem, although they are all books. So, when a person picks up a Gospel account to read, what does he or she expect? History? Biography? Myth? Theology? In short, the Gospels reflect biographical and historical information, but there is also a third concern: theology. What we have in the four Gospel accounts, according to Craig L. Blomberg in *Jesus and the Gospels*, is a "theological biography."

Although there is a general chronological progression in the Gospels from Jesus' birth to his death and resurrection, the Gospels are designed to communicate theologically through thematic and topical arrangements. Readers who demand that all four Gospels be exactly chronological are imposing an illegitimate standard. To read one of the four Gospels correctly requires accepting its topical and thematic arrangement.

When we open the Gospel of Mark, believed to be "Peter's Memoirs" recorded by John Mark (Acts 12:12), we are bombarded with story after story after story. While reading along at this rapid pace, we find that Mark arranges his material topically, weaving certain themes in and out of his "theological biography." In Mark 1:14-39, Jesus calls his first disciples, drives out an evil spirit, heals many from disease, and seeks solitude. Immediately following this, in Mark 1:40—2:17, Jesus heals a leprous man and a paralytic,

the grocery store—they'll work just fine.) Put all of the nature objects in a bucket. You'll also need enough aluminum foil for each student to have a piece about a foot long. Gather tape, glue, markers, and the poster or cardboard for students to use in the concluding activity. If you'd like, you may also want to include other art supplies such as yarn, glitter, watercolors, or magazines. If you'll be playing music during the final activity, set up the CD player and cue the CD.

CONNECTION

Welcome students to the Bible study and start things off with this mind-bending mixer.

calls Levi to be his disciple, and teaches. In Mark 3:7-34, Jesus seeks solitude, calls the rest of his 12 disciples, teaches, and makes a statement on discipleship. By the time we reach 4:35, Mark has already established several major themes: discipleship, Christ's solitude, Christ's teachings, and—most prominently— Christ's authority over human illness and demonic powers. Mark then goes on to build upon this theme: Jesus not only continues to display his authority over human life and demonic powers but also over the natural world.

Mark's focus and emphasis on Jesus' miracles is intentional. If we accept the widely held idea that Mark originally wrote his Gospel primarily to a Roman Christian audience that was severely persecuted under Nero, we can see the purpose of that emphasis. Reading about Jesus' authority over demonic powers, human disease, and the raging sea would certainly instill a sense of bold confidence and resilient faith in that downtrodden community. And that is the point. Jesus never performed miracles for his own sake; the Gospel of Mark emphasizes that miracles were meant to build faith in Jesus' followers.

When the Pharisees asked Jesus for a sign in Mark 8:11, Jesus refused the request. But where the faith of his disciples was concerned, Jesus offered plenty of reasons to believe. The circumstances surrounding his birth, the testimony of John the Baptist, his authoritative teaching, and his miracles were all meant to enable his followers to trust that he was the Christ. The miracles finally led to Peter's confession in Mark 8:29 (see study 6), but at the time it seemed that the only ones in these miracle accounts who clearly recognized Jesus for who he was were the demons; in 5:7 Legion cries, "What do you want with me, Jesus, Son of the Most High?"

Have youth sit in a circle on the floor. Pass out slips of paper and pens, and tell teenagers that you're going to have them creatively finish a sentence and write their endings on their slips of paper. Clarify that what they write should be totally made up and can be serious or funny. Also instruct them to keep their answers confidential. They should not write their name

LEADER TIP

This game works best with groups of 8-12 students. If you have more than 12 participants, divide students into smaller groups; each small group can play its own game.

on their slip nor should they let anyone else know what they wrote.

When everybody understands the rules, read the sentence students are to complete: **It's a miracle! Last night…**

(If youth need help, suggest a few ideas such as "It's a miracle! Last night my dog flew to Mars!" or "It's a miracle! Last night the Cubs won the World Series!")

Once all students have written their sentence, have them fold their slips of paper and pass them to you.

Now explain how the game will work. Say:

The goal of the game is to correctly guess what others wrote. I will start the game by reading all of the answers aloud twice. I'll read the sentences only these two times—you must do your best to remember all of them.

Read the sentences twice. Go ahead and chuckle at the funny answers! This will set the tone for how hilarious this game can be.

After you've read the sentences, have students take turns going around the circle and guessing who said what. Designate one student to go first. He or she may say something like, "Nathan, did you say, 'It's a miracle! Last night I grew 2 feet taller'?"

The player who has been guessed (Nathan, in this case) must either admit or deny that he wrote that completion. Tell students that they must be truthful.

If the answer is "no," then the guessing player's turn ends and the next person in the circle gets to take a guess.

However, if the player guessed correctly, the guessed student must get up from his seat and sit beside the guessing player. The guessed player is now "out" of the game in the sense that he no longer gets a turn to make guesses. However, he is now part of the guessing player's team and should work to assist that team captain in making future guesses.

Whenever a player makes a correct guess, he or she gets another turn. That person may continue guessing until making an incorrect guess. Have students continue this pattern of guessing around the circle.

If a student guesses a team captain's sentence completion, then the team captain and all of his or her team must go sit by the player who guessed their captain's answer. They now all belong to the new player's team.

The game ends either when one person accumulates all the players on his or her team or when one player remains whose answer has not been correctly guessed.

Ask students if they have any questions—but explain that they'll catch on easily as they start to play. Help them start things out by directing when people are to join others' teams and so on. If youth get to the point where they can't remember the remaining answers, you may want to give them hints or reread the answers to the group a final time—it's up to you.

After the game,

Ask: **How were you able to guess the person behind each make-believe miracle?**

Say: **Today we're going to look more closely at Jesus' miracles and what they demonstrate about his identity.**

LEADER TIP

This game can easily become a youth group favorite! Use it on retreats or fun nights and try different starters such as the following:

- If I wrote an autobiography, its title would be...

- I made up a new breakfast cereal with a special ingredient; the cereal is called...and its secret ingredient is...

- If I were a superhero, my name would be...

- The best TV show of all time is...

EXPLORATION

Share some of the details you learned from the Leader Insight about the organization of the Gospels and how the authors often wrote using an arrangement of events based on their theological emphases. Then say: **John Mark is the author of the second Gospel, likely using Peter as his source of information. It is thought that he wrote his Gospel during the time of Nero, when Christians were severely persecuted for their faith. As we study Jesus' miracles in the book of Mark, keep this question in mind: How did the persecution his readers faced influence what Mark emphasized in his Gospel?**

Assign one third of the students to skim Mark 1:14-39, the second third to skim Mark 1:40–2:17, and the final third to skim Mark 3:7-34. Pass out paper and prompt students to write quick notes about the major events and key themes in the chapters they've skimmed.

After three to five minutes, have a volunteer for each chapter briefly share the highlights of that passage. Help students see the repeated themes.

Once the basic events and themes have been summed up, prompt teenagers to form groups of four. Say: **Set aside what you already know of Jesus. Imagine you were reading Mark's Gospel for the first time, as a first-century Christian.**

Ask: **What would you be thinking so far about Jesus? Why?**
• **How would the events so far (as recorded in Mark) have affected you? Why?**

Now, ask students to import themselves into the story as one of the disciples. Invite a volunteer to read aloud Mark 4:35-41 while everyone else reads along. Then ask foursomes:

• **If you were one of the disciples, what might have been your thoughts and feelings during the storm?**

• **What might have been your thoughts and feelings about Jesus?**

• **Why were the disciples terrified in Mark 4:41? What do you think was going through their heads?**

Explain to groups that Mark 4:41 is, in essence, the thesis of the upcoming chapters. Say: **The disciples asked, "Who is this? Even the winds and waves obey him!" Though they had already seen Jesus perform several miracles, this powerful miracle absolutely stunned them. His words calmed a raging storm! Suddenly they knew they were following more than just a dynamic preacher.**

Mark highlights the disciples' question "Who is this?" and then immediately follows up with another miracle account.

Invite a few volunteers to read aloud Mark 5:1-20, then have foursomes discuss:

- **If you were a disciple present during this event, what would you have thought or felt?**

- **Compare this event to the previous incident. How is it similar? How is it different? If you were a disciple, how would this event affect your understanding of Jesus' identity?**

When they're done discussing, say: **Surprisingly, it was the *demons* who acknowledged Jesus' authority. He was God! Now, you'll each study two more miracles that provide further insight into Jesus' identity and the meaning of his miracles.**

Instruct foursomes to break into two pairs, a pair A and a pair B. Direct all the A's to go to one side of the room and all the B's to go to the other side. Explain that each side of the room will now study two of Jesus' miracles using an inductive Bible study guide in their Student Journals on pages 26-27. Let them know that they'll be responsible for teaching others what they've learned, so challenge them to take copious notes.

Assign group A the miracle of the dead girl and the miracle of the sick woman in Mark 5:21-43.

Assign group B Jesus' feeding of the 5,000 and Jesus walking on water in Mark 6:30-51.

Tell students to follow the directions in their Student Journals. Walk around and observe while they work, helping students who need guidance. Give students about 20 minutes for their inductive study.

Once the time is up, direct everyone to return to their original foursomes. The A pair in each foursome should then explain to the B pair what they studied and what conclusions they drew, and vice versa. As students work to teach each other, prompt them to share specific insights from their notes as well as parts of the miracle accounts that were personally meaningful to them.

When teenagers have finished discussing their Bible passages, have everyone gather back together and sit in a circle. Sum things up by saying: **Jesus displayed his authority and power over life and death, sickness and disease, angels and demons, nature...over all of the created world.**

TRANSFORMATION

·······If you'd like, play worship music quietly on a CD player during this concluding section of the study.

Pass around the bucket containing small objects from nature so each teenager can take one. Ask students to hold the object and prayerfully consider these questions:

- **How does the reality that Jesus has power and authority over all nature—the land, the water, the stars, the weather— affect your outlook on your present circumstances?**

- **How will you live in a way that recognizes the reality of Jesus' power and authority over all of nature?**

After a few minutes, direct youth to turn to a partner and discuss their answers to the questions. Challenge them to each commit to one specific action step.

Next, pass around the aluminum foil. Ask teenagers to each tear a foot-long piece of foil from the roll. Instruct students to look into the dull reflection of their face in the foil and take a moment to silently ponder these questions:

- **How does the reality that Jesus has power and authority _over your own life_—your health, your safety, your relationships—influence your outlook on your circumstances?**

- **How will you live in a way that recognizes the reality of Jesus' power and authority over your own life?**

Again, have youth share their answers with a partner, focusing on a specific action step they can take. Have pairs pray for each other, praising God for his power and committing to their action steps as ways to honor God's authority in their lives.

When they're done praying, set out the poster board, scissors, extra nature objects, tape, glue, and any other art supplies you gathered. Prompt students to work together to create a poster that represents Jesus' power and authority over all things. They should include all of their nature objects and foil pieces on the poster. (If they need help, you could suggest ideas like using the objects and foil to create mountains or a map, or to spell out meaningful words from the study. The possibilities are endless!)

When students are done with their poster, congratulate them on their creativity and wrap up the study by saying: **This poster you made is a visual representation of the prayers you just prayed, recognizing Jesus as the ultimate power and authority in your life and in this world.**

> ## LEADER TIP
>
> You may want to give students a preview of next week's study by saying the following: **In the passages we just studied, only the demons seemed to recognize who Jesus really was. Next week we're going to see when the disciples finally started to "get it" and to understand Jesus' true authority and identity.**
>
> Also, point out the Study 5 "On Your Own" section in the Student Journals on page 25, and encourage teenagers to use the personal Bible study and reflection suggestions in their devotional time during the week.

The Recognition—Jesus' Identity and Mission

●●

Scripture Focus: Psalm 63:1-4; Matthew 4:19; 16:1; 16:13-26; 17:1-8; 20:28; John 6:47-48, 51; 10:14-18; 14:6; 17:3
Supplies: Bibles; Student Journals; pens or pencils; photocopies of "Opinions About Jesus" handout (p. 65), 1 per student; Third Day's *Come Together* CD or Crystal Lewis' *Beauty for Ashes* CD (optional); CD player (optional); photocopies of "Worship Responsive Reading" (pp. 66-67), 1 per student

●●

> *"Today, everyone has an opinion about Jesus, and these opinions range from the traditional to the novel to the heretical…The earnest seeker of truth should move beyond a subjective image of Jesus toward an objective knowledge of who he really is."*
>
> —Douglas Groothuis, ***Jesus in an Age of Controversy***

PREPARATION

Before the meeting, read the Leader Insight section to dive deeper into the topic of Peter's confession and Jesus' transfiguration. Then read through the study to familiarize yourself with the Scripture passages and activities.

For the **Exploration** section, photocopy the "Opinions About Jesus" handout (p. 65), making one copy for each student. Also consider doing the optional activity of showing a video you've created. Simply go to a mall, a high school sporting event, or another teenage hangout. Find 5 to 10 teenagers who are willing to let you videotape their answer to this question: "What is your opinion about Jesus?" Do your best to make

LEADER INSIGHT

The events in Matthew 16:13—17:13 are pivotal in Jesus' ministry, for it is here that his identity is recognized, his mission is declared, and his true glory is revealed. When Jesus asks his disciples in Matthew 16:13, "Who do people say the Son of Man is?" we get a glimpse into Jesus' popularity. Common opinion equated Jesus with great and highly revered prophets like Elijah and Jeremiah. These estimations of Jesus indicated that at this point in his ministry most of the public recognized his power and the truth of his teachings.

Yet it is Peter who first boldly proclaimed the true identity of Jesus as the Christ. *Christos* in the Greek is equivalent to the Hebrew word *Messiah*, which means "anointed one." Peter declared Jesus to be the fulfillment of prophecies, the Messiah of God sent to deliver his people Israel. Peter's declaration was more than a logical deduction based on the events and miracles he had observed—it was a spiritual understanding revealed to him by God (Matthew 16:17). It's important to note that Peter's understanding of Jesus' identity *preceded* his glimpse at Jesus' glory in the Transfiguration, in sharp contrast to the Pharisees and Sadducees who demanded a sign from heaven (Matthew 16:1).

Jesus praised Peter for his faith, calling him "the rock." In essence, as Craig L. Blomberg put it in *Jesus and the Gospels*, "Peter has just told Jesus who he is; now Jesus tells Peter who he is." Yet soon after this event, Peter's inability to understand and support Jesus' true mission prompted Jesus to reproach

sure that most of the kids who answer the question *are not Christians*. The goal is to have a short homemade video that represents common opinions about Jesus.

For the **Transformation** activity, make photocopies of the "Worship Responsive Reading" handout (pp. 66-67); you'll need one copy for every participant, including any adult leaders. If you're able to track down the Crystal Lewis *Beauty for Ashes* CD or the Third Day *Come Together* CD, you'll want to set up a CD player with one of those CDs ready to play the song "The Lion and the Lamb" (Lewis) or "Show Me Your Glory" (Third Day).

CONNECTION

Energetically greet teenagers as they arrive, then launch the study by having students discuss these questions in pairs or trios. Ask:

him, calling him "Satan." As Blomberg clarifies, "[Jesus] is not saying Peter was possessed by demons, but he is very seriously stressing that Peter is reflecting the same perspective as the devil, who wanted to keep Christ from the road to the cross." With great passion, Jesus asserted his determination to follow through on his mission: to go to the cross, to suffer, and to die for the redemption of humankind.

Just six days after being called "Satan," Peter, along with James and John, experienced a divine confirmation that Jesus is the Christ when they saw Jesus transfigured (Matthew 17:1-13). Jesus appeared in a glorified state along with Moses and Elijah. The presence of Moses, symbolizing "the law," and Elijah, symbolizing "the prophets," signified to the disciples (and to us) that Jesus, the Christ, was in fact the whole *point* of the law and the prophets.

Students will likely recognize the words of the Father in Jesus' transfiguration: "This is my Son, whom I love; with him I am well pleased." These are the same words the Father spoke when Jesus was baptized (see Study 3), but this time he added the phrase, "Listen to him!" This command hearkens back to Deuteronomy 18:15-19 when God told his people he'd be sending a great prophet and directed them to listen to him. With his divine command, God the Father confirmed Peter's declaration that Jesus is the promised Christ, prophesied in ages past.

- **When you were a kid, what was a funny nickname you called a brother or sister?**
- **What was an affectionate nickname someone in your family had for you?**
- **What about name-calling? What nicknames did other kids call you in a joking or mean-spirited way?**
- **What is the meanest childhood nickname you've ever heard of?**

When they're done, share a story from your own childhood—either of a nickname other kids or siblings called you or a name you used to call someone else. Then say: **Name-calling can be funny, but it can also really hurt. Imagine how Peter felt when Jesus called him about the worst nickname in the book!**

Read the following (excerpted from Matthew 16:23): **Jesus turned and said to Peter, "Get behind me, Satan!**

Say: **Why in the world would Jesus call Peter, one of his lead disciples, *Satan*? Seems a little extreme, doesn't it? Let's dive into our study—and you'll soon find out why Jesus spoke to Peter that way.**

EXPLORATION

Ready aloud Matthew 16:13, then say: **Jesus asked his disciples who people thought he was. Let's look at some common opinions about Jesus.**

Have students form groups of three to five, and pass out photocopies of the "Opinions About Jesus" handout (p. 65) you prepared before the study, one per student. Teenagers should read the quotes from both Christian and secular sources aloud in their groups, then discuss these questions (also printed on the handout):

- **Which of these opinions about Jesus is most common?**

- **Which opinion surprised you or was the most interesting to you? Why?**

- **What are other common perceptions of Jesus?**

When small groups are done with their discussion, invite them to share highlights of their conclusions. Then say: **We've looked at what contemporary opinions are of Jesus. Who did people in *his* time say that he was?** Invite a volunteer to read aloud Matthew 16:14.

Say: **Though these answers are pretty different from the opinions people today have about Jesus, when we realize their meaning, they tell us a lot about Jesus' reputation.**

LEADER TIP

Another fun option to start out this study is to get a baby name book from your local library. Before teenagers arrive, look up the meanings of several of the names of students in your group (the more bizarre, the better).

Start out the study by reading the various name meanings and having kids guess whose name each meaning matches. (Instruct kids who know their own name meanings to keep quiet.) After you've gone through the names you prepared, continue with the activity as outlined here.

Explain to the group that Elijah, Jeremiah, and John the Baptist were great heroes to the people—they were representatives of God who spoke God's truth with great power and authority. The fact that many people thought Jesus was one of these people—or was *like* one of these people—indicates that Jesus was very popular and highly regarded.

Ask:

- **What common threads can you find between the people's opinion of Jesus and current opinions about Jesus?**

VIDEO OPTION

If you were able to create the video described in the Preparation section, play it for the group once they've finished discussing the quotes on the "Opinions About Jesus" handout. Explain that it is a video of random teenagers who you simply asked, "What is your opinion about Jesus?" After the video, prompt youth to form small groups and discuss these questions:

- Which of these opinions about Jesus is most common?
- Which opinion surprised you or was the most interesting to you? Why?
- What are other common perceptions of Jesus?

(Encourage kids to refer to the quotations on their handouts.)

Say: **As we saw in last week's study, it seems that up to this point the disciples hadn't yet decisively answered this question for themselves—they still seemed confused about Jesus' true identity. This time, Jesus didn't let his disciples off the hook.**

Invite a volunteer to read aloud Matthew 16:15-16.

Ask:

- **How do you imagine the other disciples reacted when they heard Peter say this?**
- **How was this a turning point for the disciples? What are the implications of Peter's declaration?**

Say: **People today are used to the term *Jesus Christ*—treating the word *Christ* as if it were Jesus' last name. When we treat the word *Christ* so casually, we really miss the point.**

Direct teenagers to return to their small groups and read the background information about the name "the Christ, the Son of the living God" on page 30 in their Student Journals.

For your convenience, here is the text found in the Student Journal:

The name "Christ" is from the Greek *Christos* and is the New Testament equivalent of the Old Testament Hebrew term that means "Messiah." Its literal meaning is "anointed," or "anointed one," and it refers to someone who was anointed as a leader, such as a priest or a king. Yet when Peter called Jesus "the Christ," he was calling him more than a leader. He was referring to Jesus as the prophesied Messiah, a coming leader of Israel from the line of David who was expected to bring about a "golden age" to Israel and to bring salvation and hope.

When Peter called Jesus "the Son of the living God," he added an extra dimension to his declaration that Jesus was the Christ. Some saw the coming Messiah as only a human leader, but Peter also acknowledged Jesus' identity as God's Son.

Ask small groups:

• **What light does this additional information shed on Peter's confession? What does Peter mean?**

• **How do you think Peter felt when he said it? Why?**

Say: **Peter insightfully confirmed Jesus' true identity as the Christ. Now let's look at the Christ and his mission.**

Direct small groups to read together Matthew 16:17-22, then discuss:

• **What does Jesus reveal about the mission of the Christ?**

• **How do Jesus' words contradict Peter's concept of the Christ?**

• **Can you sympathize with Peter? What might have been his reasons for disagreeing with Jesus?**

Prompt groups to read Matthew 16:23, then discuss:

• **Why did Jesus call Peter "Satan"? Was he being extreme? Explain.**

• **Did Jesus mean that Peter was possessed? Why or why not?**

• **What relationship might Satan have had to Peter's declaration that he would never let Jesus be killed?**

Gather the group back together and invite small groups to share their conclusions about why Jesus called Peter "Satan." Then say: **It's only natural to sympathize with Peter. After all, he loved Jesus dearly, so of course he didn't want him to be killed. He had also just called Jesus "the Christ"—identifying him as the Messiah. Peter was understandably confused by Jesus' declaration that he would be murdered.**

Jesus' harsh words for Peter were not because Jesus was being mean; he used extreme language because Peter was trying to deter Jesus from his Messianic mission. Satan wanted to prevent Jesus from going to the cross. When Peter rebuked Jesus, his words lined up exactly with Satan's ultimate goal—preventing Jesus' sacrificial death for the sins of the world.

Direct youth to take their Student Journals, Bibles, and pens and spread out in the room so that they can each have their own space. Prompt them to turn to "Peter's Journal" on page 31. Say: **Step into Peter's shoes for a moment—how do you think he was feeling at that point? He just declared Jesus to be the Christ, then moments later Jesus says he's going to be killed! Take a moment to imagine how Peter was likely feeling and write a short journal entry as if you were Peter.**

Prompt students to take three to five minutes to write in "Journal Entry 1." When time's up, read aloud Matthew 17:1-8 while students read along in their Bibles. Say: **What a roller coaster week for Peter! Just six days after Jesus said he would be killed and called Peter "Satan," he saw Jesus transfigured in all his glory.**

> **LEADER TIP**
>
> Point out the Study 6 "On Your Own" section in the Student Journals on page 29, and encourage teenagers to use the personal Bible study and reflection suggestions in their devotional time during the week.

Have teenagers again step into Peter's shoes and write a second journal entry, imagining what Peter might be thinking or feeling after the Transfiguration.

After three to five minutes, gather everyone back together and invite a few volunteers to share their journal entries. Then ask the group:

• **Why do you think Jesus revealed his glory to Peter, James, and John?**

Invite a volunteer to read aloud Matthew 16:1, then ask:

• **The Pharisees and Sadducees asked for a sign from heaven, but Jesus refused. Why do you think he chose instead to show this "sign" to the three disciples?**

TRANSFORMATION

Say: **Let's go back to the critical question Jesus asked Peter: "Who do you say that I am?" In our culture it's not popular to really and truly believe that Jesus is God!**

Have students lie facedown on the ground as the disciples did in the transfiguration account. Direct them to silently and prayerfully reflect on the question, "Who do *you* say that I am?" Challenge students to evaluate if they lean toward popular secular opinions about Jesus—that he was just a good teacher—or do they, like Peter, believe he is the Christ?

If you're able, play the song "The Lion and the Lamb" from Crystal Lewis' album *Beauty for Ashes* or "Show Me Your Glory" from Third Day's *Come Together* while teenagers are praying.

Conclude the time of reflection by inviting students to sit up and worship God with a responsive reading. Distribute the "Worship Responsive Reading" handouts (pp. 66-67), and tell youth and other adult leaders to follow the directions and read aloud together their parts as indicated (for example, *all* males should read the parts designated "Boys"). You should read the part designated "Leader."

LEADER TIP

Just a reminder that in Study 12, you'll need to pass out a bunch of newspapers from a variety of dates, so keep collecting them (or if you haven't started yet, start now).

Opinions About Jesus

"Jesus was a brilliant Jewish stand-up comedian, a phenomenal improvisor. His parables are great one-liners." —Camille Paglia

"Many Wiccans acknowledge Jesus as a prophet or Enlightened Being. These individuals honor Jesus as they would any of the other great spiritual prophets, including, but not limited to: Mohammed, Moses, Krishna, and Buddha." —Coven of the Rowen Star Web site

"Millions of people claim they belong to the Christian religion, but few of them know anything about the alleged life of the founder of their religion, a mythical fellow named Jesus...Jesus is a myth just like all the other saviors and gods of old." —American Atheists Web site

"The essence of Christianity...is summed up in one mind-boggling sentence: *Jesus Christ is God* (see John 10:30). Not just part of God, or just sent by God, or just related to God. *He was* (and therefore, of course, *is*) *God*." —Charles W. Colson, *Born Again*

"Lycurgus, Numa, Moses, Jesus Christ, Mohammed, all these great rogues, all these great thought-tyrants, knew how to associate the divinities they fabricated with their own boundless ambition." —the character Dolmancé in the Marquis de Sade's "Dialogue the Fifth"

"We know God only through Jesus Christ. Without this mediator all communication with God is broken off. Through Jesus we know God. All those who have claimed to know God and prove his existence without Jesus Christ have only had futile proofs to offer." —Blaise Pascal, *Pensées*

"Both Socrates and Jesus were outstanding teachers; both of them urged and practiced great simplicity of life; both were regarded as traitors to the religion of their community; neither of them wrote anything; both of them were executed; and both have become the subject of traditions that are difficult or impossible to harmonize." —Jaroslav Pelikan, *Jesus Through the Centuries*

Discuss these questions:

- **Which of these opinions about Jesus is most common?**
- **Which opinion surprised you or was the most interesting to you? Why?**
- **What are other common perceptions of Jesus?**

Worship Responsive Reading

Read your parts aloud together as indicated.

Leader: After six days Jesus took with him Peter, James, and John the brother of James, and led them up a high mountain by themselves. There he was transfigured before them. His face shone like the sun, and his clothes became as white as the light. Just then there appeared before them Moses and Elijah, talking with Jesus.

Girls: Peter said to Jesus, "Lord, it is good for us to be here. If you wish, I will put up three shelters—one for you, one for Moses and one for Elijah."

Boys: While he was still speaking, a bright cloud enveloped them, and a voice from the cloud said, "This is my Son, whom I love; with him I am well pleased. Listen to him!"

All: Listen to him!

Leader: These are the words of Jesus...

Boys: "Come, follow me, and I will make you fishers of men."

Girls: "I am the bread of life. I am the living bread that came down from heaven. If anyone eats of this bread, he will live forever. This bread is my flesh, which I will give for the life of the world."

Adults: "I am the good shepherd; I know my sheep and my sheep know me....and I lay down my life for the sheep. No one takes it from me, but I lay it down of my own accord."

Leader: "The Son of Man did not come to be served, but to serve, and to give his life as a ransom for many."

Teenagers: "I am the way and the truth and the life. No one comes to the Father except through me."

Leader: "I tell you the truth, he who believes has everlasting life."

All: "Now this is eternal life: that they may know you, the only true God, and Jesus Christ, whom you have sent."

Leader: When the disciples saw you in your glory, they fell on their faces and worshipped you. We also worship you!

Girls: "O God, you are my God, earnestly I seek you; my soul thirsts for you, my body longs for you, in a dry and weary land where there is no water."

Boys: "I have seen you in the sanctuary and beheld your power and your glory. Because your love is better than life, my lips will glorify you."

All: "I will praise you as long as I live, and in your name I will lift up my hands."

Leader: Jesus, you asked Peter who he believed you were. We praise you with the words of Peter.

All: "You are the Christ, the Son of the living God." Amen.

(This responsive reading is drawn from Psalm 63:1-4; Matthew 4:19; 16:16; 17:1-5; 20:28; John 6:47-48, 51; 10:14-18; 14:6; and 17:3.)

Study 7

The Stone or the Cross?

Scripture Focus: Exodus 3:14; 20:8-11; 31:15; Leviticus 24:16; Isaiah 56:7; Jeremiah 7:11; Daniel 7:13-14; Matthew 12:1-14; 16:24-26; Mark 11:15-19; Luke 4:14-30; 19:45-48; John 3:1-21; 5:18; 8:48-59; 10:22-39; 19:38-42

Supplies: Bibles; Student Journals; pens or pencils; photocopies of "Stone or Cross Study Outlines" (pp. 78-79), cut apart; 1 small, flat stone per student; permanent markers; *The Christ: His Passion* CD (optional); CD player (optional)

> *"Really, if Jesus of Nazareth was not Christ, He must have been Antichrist."*
> —G.K. Chesterton, **Orthodoxy**

PREPARATION

Before the meeting, read the Leader Insight section to dive deeper into the topic of Jesus' claims to be God and the reactions of the Pharisees and disciples. Then read through the study to familiarize yourself with the Scripture passages and activities.

For the **Exploration** activity, you'll need to make several photocopies of the "Stone or Cross Study Outlines" handout on pages 78-79. Cut apart the instruction sets. You'll need one set of instructions for every student and an equal amount of each numbered section on the handout.

You'll also need to collect stones, one per student. They should be small enough to fit in the palm of a student's hand. Later in the study, students will write on the stones, so try to pick ones that are relatively flat and smooth. You can probably find these in your yard, near a riverbed, in a field, or at a landscaping store.

If a man walked into Times Square and declared "I am Elvis Presley," and was serious, one would quickly come to the conclusion either that he had escaped from a lunatic asylum or that he was in fact "the King." One or the other must be true. What happens when a man claims to be *God*? The stakes are raised, and examining that claim becomes imperative. This is the situation we inevitably come to when we discuss the person of Jesus.

In Luke 4:18, Jesus essentially calls himself "the anointed one" (see Leader Insight for Study 3 on pages 30-31) when he states, "The Spirit of the Lord is on me." In Matthew 26:63-64 he answers affirmatively to the charge, "Tell us if you are the Christ." In the same passage he also accepts the title "Son of God." In John 8:58 Jesus claims, "Before Abraham was born, I am!" This is a clear reference to Exodus 3:14. On several occasions, including Matthew 12:8; 16:27-28; and John 3:13-14, Jesus calls himself "the Son of Man," evoking the prophetic "son of man" from Daniel 7:13.

Clearly, Jesus claimed to be God. As G.K. Chesterton wrote in *Orthodoxy*, "Really, if Jesus of Nazareth was not Christ, He must have been Antichrist." C.S. Lewis builds on Chesterton's point, writing in *Mere Christianity*, "[A man who said the sort of things Jesus said] would either be a lunatic...or else he

If you're able to acquire *The Christ: His Passion* CD, set up the CD player and cue the CD to play the song "Yes I Will" when indicated in this study outline.

CONNECTION

Warmly welcome everyone as they arrive, then start things off by having youth form groups of four. Direct them to turn to the case studies on pages 34-35 in their Student Journals. Foursomes should assign numbers within their group: 1, 2, 3, and 4. Then have them divvy up the case studies by number so that each student reads one. Have them take a moment to silently read their case study, then take turns in their foursome retelling the case studies in their own words.

For your convenience, here is a brief overview of the case studies in the Student Journal.

would be the Devil of Hell...Let us not come with any patronising nonsense about His being a great human teacher. He has not left that open to us. He did not intend to." We don't have the options of indifference or laxity: We must contend with Jesus' claims and accept them or reject them.

This is the familiar "Lord, Lunatic, Liar" defense of Jesus popularized by C. S. Lewis. Though this discussion is usually meant to force an unbeliever to deal with the actual claims of Christ, there is an additional dimension to the claim that is often overlooked.

If a person today concludes that Jesus is either a lunatic or a liar, it is quite obvious where this conclusion leads: rejection of Christianity. For the Jewish audience of Jesus' day, it also meant stoning him for blasphemy. But what if a person concludes Jesus to be Lord? What next? Jesus makes it clear: "If anyone would come after me, he must deny himself and take up his cross and follow me" (Matthew 16:25). That is the only option left.

For the disciples, this command must have seemed strange because Jesus himself had not yet approached the cross. Yet Jesus is clear that taking up the cross and following him was the evidence of one's fully convinced belief—and it still is today.

Case Study 1 examines the life of Marshall Herff Applewhite, who led the "Heaven's Gate" cult. This group committed suicide to allow their spirits to meet an alien spaceship they believed was hiding behind a comet.

Case Study 2 looks at Jim Jones, whose "Jonestown" cult committed mass suicide in their compound in Guyana. Over 900 people, including Jones, were found dead.

Case Study 3 examines the life of Shoko Asahara, an imprisoned Japanese cult leader. His followers were responsible for the Tokyo subway nerve gas attack in 1995.

Case Study 4 looks at David Koresh, once the leader of the Branch Davidians in Waco, Texas. Koresh and over 70 group members died in a siege on their compound.

Once they've heard all the case studies, have foursomes discuss these questions:

- **What stands out to you the most from these case studies? Why?**
- **What was outrageous about each cult leader's claims?**
- **How did he lead people astray?**
- **How would you have felt if someone from your family or your church joined one of these cults?**
- **What would you do or say to prevent that from happening?**

Have foursomes decide together which cult leader from the case studies was the *weirdest* and which cult leader from the four was the *most dangerous*.

When foursomes have wrapped up their discussion, have everybody gather back together. Invite groups to share thoughts from their discussion, then tally up the results for "weirdest" and "most dangerous" based on the conclusions of each foursome. Once you've determined which cult leader got the most votes for each of these categories, ask:

- **Why was _____ the weirdest? Explain.**
- **What made _____ so dangerous? Explain.**

> ## LEADER TIP
>
> In Luke 4:18-19, Jesus reads Isaiah 61:1-2a, one of the passages the students learned about in Study 1 (pp. 9-18). Help students make the connection to what they learned regarding the servant and king Isaiah prophesied about. You can also make a second connection to Study 3. Jesus' words "The Spirit of the Lord is upon me" closely follow Jesus' baptism, where the Spirit "descended upon him like a dove" (see Leader Insight from Study 3).

EXPLORATION

Say: **Let's look at another case.**

Invite a volunteer to read aloud Luke 4:14-21, then ask:

- **Where have you heard this before?**
- **What does this mean? What is Jesus claiming?**

Say: **Let's look at how Jesus' hometown synagogue responded to his claim.**

Invite another volunteer to read aloud Luke 4:22-30, then say: **Not only did they not believe Jesus' claim, but they were so upset that they wanted to kill him by throwing him over a cliff!**

Many religious leaders in Jesus' time viewed Jesus as dangerous, for much the same reason we view the four cult leaders we just discussed as outrageous and dangerous. The New Testament religious leaders not only thought it was ridiculous and offensive for Jesus to call himself "God," they believed it was blasphemous. They were ready to defend and protect their "faith" at all costs.

Instruct foursomes to divide up using their assigned number: designate an area of the room for all the 1s to go, an area for all the 2s to go, and so on. Explain that in their new groups, students will work together to study an incident in which Jesus' actions and claims were extremely offensive to the religious leaders—so offensive, in fact, that they sought to kill him!

Distribute the "Stone or Cross Study Outlines" instructions to each corresponding group, giving one set of instructions for each student. Direct students to turn to pages 36-37 in their Student Journals, where they can record their answers and any other notes from their discussion. Explain that groups will have about 15 minutes to do an in-depth study of the passage, to take notes, and to be prepared to present their information to others.

> For your convenience, here is an overview of what each group will be studying:
> *Group 1:* Exodus 20:8-11; 31:15; Matthew 12:1-14; John 5:18
> *Group 2:* Isaiah 56:7; Jeremiah 7:11; Mark 11:15-19; Luke 19:45-48
> *Group 3:* Exodus 3:14; John 8:48-59
> *Group 4:* Leviticus 24:16; John 10:22-39

Once 15 minutes have passed, prompt students to return to their original foursomes and take a few minutes to explain their notes and the event they studied.

Gather everyone back together and ask:

- **What stood out to you from these events?**

- **How did researching the Old Testament shed new light on Jesus' actions and how they were perceived?**

Say: **What Jesus said and did was radical and controversial. If you were a God-fearing Jew living during Jesus' time, it was appropriate to be enraged by a person's claims to be God. It was downright blasphemy!**

Ask:

- **Do you feel any sympathy for the Pharisees? Can you see where they were coming from? Explain.**

Prompt everybody to gather in a circle around the pile of stones you set out before the study. Say: **It was very clear to the people in his time that Jesus was claiming to be God. There was no middle ground. People were left with only one choice—kill him for blasphemy or believe him.**

We've just studied the first choice—the people who wanted to kill Jesus for blasphemy. Now let's look more closely at the second option.

Explain to the group that not all of the religious leaders were angry at Jesus. One in particular, Nicodemus, was curious about Jesus and was open to learning more about him. He came to Jesus one night and acknowledged that he believed Jesus was a great teacher who had come from God.

Invite a volunteer to read aloud the conversation between Jesus and Nicodemus in John 3:1-21. Reread 3:13, then invite another volunteer to read aloud Daniel 7:13-14 to provide some Old Testament context for this passage.

Ask: **What similarities do you find in these two passages?**

Summarize their thoughts by saying: **In John 3:13 Jesus identifies himself as the "Son of Man" who came from "heaven," the same "son of man, coming with the clouds of heaven" in Daniel 7:13.**

How was Nicodemus' response to Jesus' claim different from that of the other religious leaders we just studied? Let's look at a clue we find in Scripture.

Ask a second volunteer to read aloud John 19:38-42, then ask:

- **What do you think this indicates about Nicodemus? Do you think he came to belief in Jesus? Explain.**

- **John 3:16 uses the word** *believe*. **What does it mean to believe in Jesus as the Son of God?**

- **How does a person come to the point of belief in Jesus?**

- **What do you think Jesus meant when he said to Nicodemus, "But whoever lives by the truth comes into the light" (3:21)?**

Say: **John 3:16 is one of the most famous verses in all of Scripture. Sometimes Christians focus on this verse about believing as if Christianity is all about having a smooth and easy life on earth and a great eternal life in heaven. But Jesus made it very clear to his followers that there is more to the story. Choosing to believe in Jesus is a total and absolute commitment. To come out into the light means accepting all that goes along with following Jesus—both the difficult and the easy.**

LEADER TIP

Nicodemus came to see Jesus at night. Some scholars speculate that this indicates Nicodemus was afraid to be seen with Jesus (though it is equally plausible that this would be the appropriate time to inquire about such matters concerning the Law). It is likely, however, that Jesus' reference to coming into the light (John 3:21) was an indirect reference to Nicodemus' visit under cover of darkness and might have been Jesus' way of contrasting Nicodemus' timid spiritual curiosity with true, bold faith. Consider pointing this out to students and asking how this possibility affects their interpretation of verse 21.

Let's look at Jesus' explanation of what it means to follow him—it takes place between Peter's confession that Jesus is the Christ and Jesus' transfiguration.

Prompt a volunteer to read aloud Matthew 16:24-26 while the rest read along in their Bibles.

Let students know that you'd like them to more closely examine Jesus' definition of belief in him—of making him Lord. Have them turn to "Following Jesus" on page 38 in their Student Journals and write the meanings of each phrase from verse 24 in their own words, writing a full sentence to explain each phrase. (Youth will work to rewrite "deny himself," "take up his cross," and "follow me.")

••••••If you're able, play the song "Yes I Will" from *The Christ: His Passion* CD while youth are working on their definitions. The lyrics of this up-beat song are an affirmation of one's commitment to follow Jesus fully.

When youth are done writing, have each find a partner and share with each other what they discovered.

TRANSFORMATION

Invite three volunteers to read their paraphrases of Matthew 16:24, using the starting language of the verse and then putting all of their sentences together.

Then reread Matthew 16:24 aloud. Afterward, say: **Just like the Pharisees and the disciples, we need to recognize that Jesus claimed to be the Son of God. We don't have the option of view-ing him as just a good guy or an important historical figure. We each must come to our own conclusion: Do you believe him or do you think he was a blasphemous liar?**

Do you fall in line behind the Pharisees and pick up a stone? Or do you follow the disciples' example and take up your cross? There's not a middle ground—either you don't believe his claims or you embrace them and put your life on the line.

Direct youth to go one at a time to the middle of the circle, pick up a flat stone, and then go back to their place and sit down. Once every-one has a stone and is seated (including you), pass around permanent markers and instruct students to use the marker to draw a cross on one side of their stone.

Then ask teenagers to close their eyes and to pray the following prayer silently with you if it fits what they're thinking. Lead them in a prayer of commitment for those who don't have a relationship with Jesus and also a prayer that will allow Christian students to pray with you to abandon the "middle ground" and focus fully on living out Matthew 16:24.

You may want to pray something like this: **Lord, you told Nicodemus that you loved the world, that you came to save the world, and that those who believe in you will have eternal life.**

Some of us have never made a faith commitment to you—a commitment of belief and trust. Some of us want to begin that relationship with you right now, and so we pray: Jesus, we believe that you were fully God and fully human. We believe you died on the cross for our sins. We believe you rose from the dead. We want to follow you. We want to know you. We want to live in the light. Forgive us for our sins and help us begin a lifelong relationship of faith and trust in you.

Others of us have a relationship with you, Jesus, but we've been ho-hum about our faith. We've hung out in the "middle ground," believing in you but not really heeding your call to deny ourselves, take up our cross, and follow you in a lifelong commitment. We've hidden our faith in the darkness. Help us start anew. We want to live in the light. Embolden us to live completely committed lives of faith.

Thank you for your love, Lord. Amen.

Instruct teenagers to take their stones home with them and set them on their nightstand or on a dresser in their room with the cross side facing up. This will serve as a reminder to both the Christian teenagers and any spiritual seekers that there is no middle ground when it comes to Jesus. They each must decide whether he was a blasphemer (who thus deserved to be killed) or the Son of God, in which case we must each daily take up our cross.

Stone or Cross Study Outlines

Group 1 Study Outline

Directions: Use these questions to guide your study and discussion. Write your notes on pages 36-37 in your Student Journal.

"But the Pharisees went out and plotted how they might kill Jesus" (Matthew 12:14).

What is the **context**? Read Matthew 12:1-14 and John 5:18.

What is the **historical background** for what happened? Read Exodus 20:8-11; 31:15.

Why did they want to kill Jesus?

Why wasn't Jesus killed?

What does this story tell us about who Jesus was?

••

Group 2 Study Outline

Directions: Use these questions to guide your study and discussion. Write your notes on pages 36-37 in your Student Journal.

"The chief priests and the teachers of the law heard this and began looking for a way to kill him, for they feared him, because the whole crowd was amazed at his teaching" (Mark 11:18).

What is the **context**? Read Mark 11:15-19 and Luke 19:45-48.

What is the **historical background** for what happened? Read Isaiah 56:7 and Jeremiah 7:11.

Why did they want to kill Jesus?

Why wasn't Jesus killed?

What does this story tell us about who Jesus was?

••

Group 3 Study Outline

Directions: Use these questions to guide your study and discussion. Write your notes on pages 36-37 in your Student Journal.

"At this, they picked up stones to stone him, but Jesus hid himself, slipping away from the temple grounds" (John 8:59).

What is the **context**? Read John 8:48-59.

What is the **historical background** for what happened? Read Exodus 3:14.

Why did they want to kill Jesus?

Why wasn't Jesus killed?

What does this story tell us about who Jesus was?

• •

Group 4 Study Outline

Directions: Use these questions to guide your study and discussion. Write your notes on pages 36-37 in your Student Journal.

"Again the Jews picked up stones to stone him, but Jesus said to them, 'I have shown you many great miracles from the Father. For which of these do you stone me?' " (John 10:31-32).

What is the **context**? Read John 10:22-39.

What is the **historical background** for what happened? Read Leviticus 24:16.

Why did they want to kill Jesus?

Why wasn't Jesus killed?

What does this story tell us about who Jesus was?

• •

LEADER TIP

You may want to tell the group that you'd like to personally talk with any students who for the first time began a faith relationship with Jesus. Invite them to talk to you after the study or to meet with you during the week.

When youth meet with you, try to answer any of their initial questions and encourage them in their commitment. Prompt them to spend daily time in prayer and study, using the "On Your Own" section of the Student Journal as a guide. You may also want to give students some of these resources from Group Publishing that will help them grow in their Christian journey:

- *The Youth Bible* (an easy-to-understand translation, includes study notes and devotions)

- *A Fresh Start* by Scott Larson (a collection of personal devotions that answer questions teenagers might have once they've made a commitment to Jesus)

- *Living the Beatitudes of Jesus* (a book of 30 meditative prayers and devotions that will help teenagers see the world from a Christian perspective)

There may also be students in your group who are not yet ready to make a commitment to Jesus. They may have questions about Christianity that are holding them back. Offer to meet with these students; do your best to answer their questions and challenge them to spend time studying daily using the "On Your Own" section of the Student Journal, keeping notes about questions or concerns they have. Remind these students that at some point they must make a choice about Jesus—the stone or the cross? They must deal with Jesus' claims to be God and decide what they believe about him. Pray with and for these students as they explore Jesus' claims and his love.

The Values of Jesus' Kingdom—Service

••

Scripture Focus: Matthew 5:38-48; 19:16-22; 19:30–20:16; 20:20-28; John 13:1-17; Philippians 2:1-7

Supplies: Bibles; Student Journals; pens or pencils; supplies for relay race (see Preparation on pages 81-84 for details); masking tape; snacks; paper signs; pennies; bowl of water; photocopies of "Hard to Serve" handout (page 90), 1 per student; tape; scissors; magazines; glue sticks (or bottles of glue); 2 pieces of poster board; CD of reflective worship music (optional); CD player (optional)

••

> *"The kingdom of God points to an inverted, upside-down way of life that challenges the prevailing social order…Kingdom values challenge the taken-for-granted social ruts and sometimes run against the dominant cultural grain…Kingdom values, rooted in the deep Love and abiding Grace of God, seed new ways of thinking and living"*
> —Donald B. Kraybill, **The Upside-Down Kingdom**

PREPARATION

Before the meeting, read the Leader Insight section to dive deeper into the topic of Jesus' kingdom and the importance of servanthood. Then read through the study to familiarize yourself with the Scripture passages and activities.

Design and set up a relay race for the **Connection** activity. You'll want to prepare for four different tasks youth will have to perform as

LEADER INSIGHT

As the Christ, the Anointed One, Jesus is a king—but what exactly is his kingdom? "The kingdom of God" is a central teaching in the New Testament, appearing 51 times in the Gospels. "The kingdom of heaven" appears an additional 31 times. Jesus began his ministry (like his cousin John), declaring, "Repent, for the kingdom of heaven is near!" (Matthew 4:17). A fundamental understanding of this central teaching is critical to a Christian's spiritual growth.

Faithful Jews awaited a Messiah who would reestablish the kingdom of Israel. But Jesus' mission was different—rather than establishing a political kingdom, he taught about a spiritual kingdom of which his followers become citizens. As John Bright wrote in *The Kingdom of God*, "The Old Testament is illumined with the hope of the coming Kingdom, and that same Kingdom lies at the heart of the New Testament as well...But in the New Testament we encounter a change: the tense is a resounding present indicative—the Kingdom is *here!*" The kingdom is *here* in the very person of Jesus himself; the mystery of the incarnation and the gift of salvation and atonement is a fulfillment of that kingdom.

Your own biblical study of "the kingdom of God" may lead you to a variety of conclusions as to what the phrase actually means. From obscure parables about mustard seeds and pearls to Jesus' teachings in the Sermon on the Mount, it immediately becomes clear that our understanding of the kingdom of God must allow for complexity and an element of mystery.

In *The Gospel of the Kingdom*, George Eldon Ladd highlights several different understandings of what the kingdom of God is and what it means. Some view it as a reference to salvation: that those who are in relationship with God have become spiritual citizens of God's kingdom. Others believe it refers to the coming apocalypse, when God will finally establish his kingdom.

Some scholars view the kingdom as the mission of the church—in essence, that it is the church's job to propagate the kingdom and kingdom

part of the race. Here are a few ideas—pick four that will work well in your setting:

Blow up a balloon, give it static by rubbing it on your head, then stick it to a wall.

Roll like a log to a marked spot on the floor.

Sink a golf putt (using a golf club, golf ball, and plastic cup taped to the floor).

Run to a specific spot and sing the alphabet backwards.

values all over the earth. Still others view the teachings on the kingdom as an archetype of an ideal human society and as a guidepost for one's understanding of God's social values.

Surely all of these theories contain truth and, as Ladd points out, the diversity of biblical teachings on the kingdom lend to this wide array of understandings. Ladd asserts, however, that a true understanding of "the kingdom of God" comes from focusing on the original meaning of the word *kingdom* in the Old Testament and New Testament.

Ladd writes that "the primary meaning of [*kingdom*]...is the rank, authority and sovereignty exercised by a king." Thus, when one views "the kingdom of God" as primarily a reference to God's authority over our lives, "we can go through the New Testament and find passage after passage where this meaning is evident, where the Kingdom is not a realm or a people but God's reign."

Therefore, when we seek first God's kingdom (Matthew 6:33), we are ultimately seeking God's authority over all aspects of our lives. And obedience to God's authority has significant ramifications as we apply Jesus' teachings.

This study focuses on one of the central teachings of Jesus: servanthood.

Servanthood means much more than doing an occasional good deed: It is an ethic that is at the heart of the kingdom. As we see from Jesus' example, servanthood means allowing oneself to be mistreated and misunderstood; it means taking on lowly positions and tasks in an attitude of humility; it means giving generously; it means placing the needs of others—even our enemies—above our own. It is a radical call, a revolutionary way of living.

As students examine this kingdom value, help them to see the connection between serving others and acknowledging Jesus as "king"; it is in obedience to Jesus' teachings about servanthood and selflessness that we grow to better recognize and understand God's authority and kingly rule in our lives and to experience the presence of his kingdom in the here and now.

Ride a tricycle to a certain spot in the room and back.

Melt an ice cube in your hand.

Look up a bizarre word in the dictionary and write down its definition.

Diaper a doll.

Select four activities that have variety, including physical tasks, silly tasks, and mental challenges. Once you've determined which activities you'll have students do, set out an adequate number of supplies in four different areas in the room and mark a starting line on the floor using masking tape.

You'll also need to get snacks that can serve as prizes (enough so each student gets one).

For the **Exploration** activities, you'll need to set up three Kingdom Values stations in your room. At station A, post a sign that reads "Station A," and set out a pile of pennies (one per student) and a bowl filled three-quarters full with water. For station B, post a sign reading "Station B," and prepare photocopies of the "Hard to Serve" handout, enough for one per student. Also set out several pairs of scissors and a roll of tape. Station B should be near a wall. For station C, post a sign reading "Station C," and set out a piece of posterboard on which students can write. List three mini-service projects at the top, such as "mow the neighbors' lawn," "pack my sister's lunch," and "clean up after youth group." Allow plenty of room for students to add lots of ideas.

If you'd like to play music while students journey through the Kingdom Values stations, select a reflective worship CD and set up the CD player.

For the **Transformation** activity, you'll need to gather several magazines that youth can look through and cut apart. Get magazines that will portray current cultural values, such as gossip/celebrity magazines and sports magazines. If possible, get one magazine for every two students, and gather several pairs of scissors and several glue sticks (or bottles of glue). Last, write out this text on a half-sheet of paper:

"Do nothing out of selfish ambition or vain conceit, but in humility consider others better than yourselves. Each of you should look not only to your own interests, but also to the interests of others.

"Your attitude should be the same as that of Christ Jesus…[who] made himself nothing, taking the very nature of a servant" (Philippians 2:3-7).

CONNECTION

Start things out with a fun and unique relay race. (If weather permits, consider having the relay race outside.) Divide the group into teams of four students and have them line up behind the starting line. Explain each of the four tasks you selected to be part of the race (see Preparation on pages 82-83), and perhaps even demonstrate each task (students will crack up!). Let groups know that the first person in each line must complete the first task, then run back to the line and give a high five to the second person. The second people will do the second task, the third will do the third, and so on. The game ends when the first team of four successfully finishes the full relay.

When everybody understands what's happening, start the game. Encourage players to cheer for their teammates as they race. When a team has won, applaud for them and continue to cheer until everybody has finished.

When the game is done, say: **And the prize goes to...**

Do a drum roll, then give treats (such as candy bars, cans of pop, or something else that's cool) to the team that *finished last*. Do it with enough bravado that you elicit moans and groans from the rest of the group.

Say: **This doesn't seem fair, does it?**

Ask:

• **Why isn't this fair?**

Say: **Let's read a parable Jesus told that also doesn't seem fair.**

Prompt relay team foursomes to read Matthew 19:30–20:16 together, then discuss:

> ## LEADER TIP
>
> If you think your group won't get into a relay race, instead play a variation of the familiar game "Rock, Paper, Scissors." After the first round is played, announce that all of the "losers" are now on the winners' teams; they must stick with the person who beat them and stand by him or her in the next round. For the second round, announce the same rule: All the losers (and their teams) are now on the winners' teams. Continue with this new rule throughout play until the final "showdown," when only two players are left to challenge each other. Have each "team" gather around their leader and cheer for him or her during the final "Rock, Paper, Scissors" challenge. When a winner has been declared, congratulate him or her, then give treats to the *losing* team. Continue with the study as written.

• **On a scale of 1 to 10, 1 being "totally unfair" and 10 being "completely fair," how would you rate the situation Jesus describes? Explain.**

• **What do you think Jesus' point is?**

- **What does it mean that the first are last and the last are first?**

While groups are discussing the parable, pass out treats to the rest of the students.

After 5 to 10 minutes, ask groups to report back, sharing what they rated the parable regarding its fairness and explaining their take on Jesus' main point.

EXPLORATION

Invite foursomes to read Matthew 20:20-28 together, and point out to them that this incident basically happens directly after the parable they just studied.

Ask foursomes to discuss:

- **Why did this family want to be the greatest?**
- **Is personal ambition—a desire to be the best—a bad thing? Why or why not?**
- **What is radical about Jesus' statement? What did he really mean?**
- **How does this passage relate to the parable we just discussed?**

Say: **Jesus is a King—and as he explained in the parable, things work a little differently in his kingdom. Today we're going to consider what it takes to truly be great in Jesus' kingdom.**

Instruct youth to form pairs, and let them know that they'll have 20 minutes to travel to the three Kingdom Values stations you've set up in the room. Let them know that they can visit the stations in any order they'd like and that they should follow the instructions in their Student Journals on pages 42-43 for each station. Make sure they each take a Bible and pen or pencil with them.

Be available to help teenagers as they work independently at the Kingdom Values stations and, if needed, wander around the room to keep students focused and on task. If you're able, play reflective worship music in the background while youth travel from station to station.

The complete instructions for the stations are printed in the Student Journals, but here is a basic summary of each study and worship activity for your convenience:

Station A

Kingdom Value: Giving generously of time, money, and talents.

Activity: Students will squeeze a penny in their hand as they read Matthew 19:16-22. They'll consider how difficult it is to be generous and will respond in a commitment to be generous by tossing the penny into a bowl of water.

Station B

Kingdom Value: Serving people who are enemies or who are hard to serve.

Activity: Teenagers will think of and discuss an "enemy"—someone who is hard to serve. They'll read Matthew 5:38-48, then write a blessing on a paper representation of the person. Students will make specific commitments of ways to serve others.

Station C

Kingdom Value: Taking action to care for the poor and needy.

Activity: Youth will study John 13:1-17, then will work together to brainstorm specific things they can do to help those in need. Each student will commit to one practical application step.

TRANSFORMATION

Give teenagers a five-minute warning, then when time is up, prompt everyone to gather together and sit with their partner. Ask:

- **What stood out to you most from the Kingdom Values stations? Why?**

- **What action step did you commit to from station C?**

Prompt pairs to read Philippians 2:1-7, then point out to students that in verse 3, the phrases "selfish ambition" and "vain conceit"

contrast directly with "humility" and considering others above one-self. Have pairs discuss the following questions. Ask:

- **What are some other "worldly values" like selfishness and vanity?**
- **What are the world's values concerning time, money, enemies, or the needy?**
- **How do these values contrast directly with kingdom values?**
- **Philippians 2:5 says that our example in humility and service is Jesus. What about Jesus do you want to imitate? How do you want to grow in your imitation of Jesus?**

Distribute magazines and scissors to pairs, and challenge students to take a few minutes to find two or three images, phrases, or words that symbolize our culture's focus on self. They should look for examples that key in on values like...

- being number one,
- amassing material possessions,
- putting your own needs first,
- focusing on superficial things, or
- being obsessed with what others think of you.

As pairs find and cut out words and images, prompt them to discuss the following questions. Ask:

- **Do you agree that it's human nature to want to be number one? Why or why not?**
- **What are examples of this that we see in society?**

As pairs finish up, have them glue their images to a poster. The group should create a collage, allowing images to overlap if needed. Do your best to make sure, though, that the words and images are all glued upright. As pairs affix their images to the poster, have volunteers explain to everyone else what images or words they chose and what they represent.

Affirm youth for their selections, and repeat any particularly strong insights. Then say: **The values of Jesus' kingdom run totally contrary to the way most people live their lives. In fact, Christian author Donald Kraybill called it "the upside-down kingdom," saying, "The kingdom of God points to an inverted, upside-down way of life that challenges the prevailing social order...Kingdom values challenge the taken-for-granted social ruts and sometimes run against the dominant cultural grain....Kingdom values, rooted in the deep Love and abiding Grace of God, seed new ways of thinking and living." Jesus' teachings turn the world's value system on its head.**

Turn the poster upside down so that all the images and words are now inverted, then use glue to affix the Philippians 2:3-5 piece of paper you prepared before the study to the middle of the poster.

Invite a volunteer to read the Scripture passage aloud, then wrap things up by having students pray with their partners regarding their commitment to serve others and live with kingdom values.

(When the glue on the poster has completely dried, hang it up in your room as a reminder to students of what they've learned from this study.)

> **LEADER TIP**
>
> Point out the Study 8 "On Your Own" section in the Student Journals on page 41, and encourage teenagers to use the personal Bible study and reflection suggestions in their devotional time during the week.

Hard to Serve

Study 9

The Values of Jesus' Kingdom—Love

••

Scripture Focus: Matthew 9:10-13; 11:19; Mark 1:40-42; Luke 7:36-50; 17:11-19; 19:1-10; John 4:1-29; 1 John 4:7-12, 20-21

Supplies: Bibles; Student Journals; pens or pencils; VCR or DVD player; *Les Misérables* video or DVD; TV; box; several random objects; blank "Hello, My Name Is" adhesive name tags; markers

••

> *"Christian love grants the beloved all his imperfections and weaknesses and in all his changes remains with him, loving the person it sees. If this were not so, Christ would never have loved, for where could he have found the perfect man!"* —Søren Kierkegaard, **Works of Love**

PREPARATION

Before the meeting, read the Leader Insight section to dive deeper into the topic of Jesus' kingdom and the importance of love. Then read through the study to familiarize yourself with the Scripture passages and activities.

For the **Connection** activity, you'll need to cue up *Les Misérables*, the 1998 film starring Liam Neeson, Geoffrey Rush, Uma Thurman, and Claire Danes. First set the VCR timer to 0:00:00 as the studio logo appears at the start of the film, then fast forward to approximately 0:32:45 when Fantine sits in jail between two guards. The scene you'll show lasts until approximately 0:35:40, when the mayor rushes to Fantine's side, yelling, "Water!" Be sure to preview this clip. (If you're working with a younger group, see the Leader Tip on page 93 that suggests an alternate scene.)

In biblical times, Jewish laws about spiritual purity were closely connected to outward actions that could cause a person to be considered "unclean."

Lepers in Jesus' time were kept out of the community, not only for health reasons but also because their skin disease made them ritually unclean; their uncleanness could "rub off on" anyone who associated with them. For this reason they were both physically and socially ostracized. As the *Zondervan Illustrated Bible Backgrounds Commentary* explains, "Leprosy, like a corpse, imparts impurity to objects found within the same enclosure (known as the principle of a tent), so the leper is like a living corpse." This phrase, "like a living corpse," is meant literally, for Jews had rigid guidelines preventing them from touching dead bodies; but it also can speak figuratively about the lives of lepers and indeed the lives of many others ostracized in New Testament society.

For the **Exploration** section, you'll need to collect lots of random objects, at least one per student. Grab objects such as kitchen utensils (mixing spoon, bowl, measuring cup, salad tongs, colander); office supplies (stapler, rubber band, eraser, white correction fluid, tape, legal pad); household tools (hammer, nail, sandpaper, yardstick); sewing supplies (needle, thread, pincushion); first-aid supplies (adhesive bandage, ointment, gauze pad); gardening tools (shovel, glove, seeds); sports equipment (tennis racket, soccer ball, catcher's mitt); or miscellaneous household items (CD, phone book, light bulb, battery, tennis shoe, blanket, hairbrush, clock). Teenagers will use these objects to create their own object lessons about Jesus' love, so select a wide variety of items. Make sure you have enough so that every student can have an object, then put them all in a big box.

For the **Transformation** activity, you'll need adhesive name tags—the commonly used ones that say "Hello" at the top, then say "My Name Is" on the second line. Your church probably has a stack of these to give to visitors; or, if needed, you can purchase these at any office supply store or most grocery stores. You'll need one for every student in your group.

CONNECTION

Greet students and start the Bible study by showing a clip from the movie *Les Misérables*. The scene begins at approximately 0:32:45 as

Many prostitutes, tax collectors, adulterous men and women, and diseased people carried out their existence as though they were the living dead—without love from friends and neighbors, feeling emotionally spent and spiritually empty. How many people today are similarly treated like the living dead by the church?

Jesus' kindness to the lepers in Mark 1:40-42 and Luke 17:11-19 exemplifies the love and grace he regularly showed to outcasts: The kingdom love of Jesus abolishes all stereotypes, steps over all boundaries, ignores all stigmas, and forgives all sin. Jesus *loved* sinners. He looked past the ugly outsides or the outrageous behavior and saw within each person a soul worth loving, worth ransoming, worth cherishing. In Jesus' kingdom, love rules...literally. For as John tells us, God—our king—is *love* (1 John 4:8).

Fantine sits in jail flanked by two guards. During this scene, the police inspector Javert decides to severely punish Fantine, a prostitute, because of a fight she had been involved in when a man put snow down her dress. Stop the clip at approximately 0:35:40, when the mayor runs to Fantine's side and yells, "Water! Water!"

After the clip, have students form trios to debrief what they just saw. Ask:

- **What's your reaction to this scene?**
- **What kind of person is the inspector?**
- **What kind of person is the mayor?**
- **How do you think the mayor's actions affected Fantine?**
- **Why is mercy so powerful?**

LEADER TIP

In the recommended scene, Fantine, who works as a prostitute, is dressed in a low-cut dress. If you're concerned that this may be a distraction to your students, show an alternate clip from the movie, starting at approximately 0:03:00, when a woman rouses a man sleeping on a bench and ending at approximately 0:05:40, when Valjean says, "In the morning I'll be a new man."

In this alternate scene, a priest shows mercy to Valjean when he is a prisoner, just released from jail. If you select this clip, modify the discussion questions accordingly by asking about the kind of person the priest is, the kind of person Valjean is, and how the priest's actions might have changed Valjean.

- **Who are you more like in your response to sinners—the inspector or the mayor? Explain.**
- **Could you say the mayor is expressing "love" to Fantine? Explain.**

EXPLORATION

Say: **Let's look at another scenario that's a lot like the one we just watched.**

Have trios study Luke 7:36-50, then discuss:

- **How is the woman like Fantine?**
- **How are Jesus' actions like the mayor's actions?**
- **What impact do you think Jesus' actions had on the woman?**
- **What makes Jesus' love radical and shocking?**

Have everyone gather back into a large group. Invite trios to share their conclusions from their discussion of the movie and the Bible story.

Say: **The mayor forgave Fantine's legal offense. Jesus forgave the woman's spiritual offense: her sin. Last week we studied serving others as one of the distinctive values of Jesus' kingdom. Today we'll study a second value that distinguishes Jesus' kingdom from the rest of culture—it is the value of love expressed in mercy and grace.**

Direct students to return to their trios, then number off by 1s, 2s, and 3s. Explain that every teenager should randomly grab an object from the box you've set in the middle of the room. Have the 1s take their objects with them to one side of the room, the 2s take their objects with them

NON-MEDIA OPTION

If for some reason you're unable to use the *Les Misérables* video, have students form trios and tell each other about a time in their childhood when they got caught doing something wrong. What happened? Who caught them? What was the consequence? Was the punishment harsher than it should have been, just right, or too mild?

If you select this option, modify the discussion questions in the Exploration section accordingly, asking students to compare their own wrong actions and the actions of the parent or authority figure who punished them to the woman's and Jesus' reactions in the story.

to the other side of the room, and the 3s take their objects with them and sit in the middle of the room. Students should also take their Bibles, Student Journals, and pens or pencils with them.

Once they form their new groups, students should put their objects in a pile and forget about them for awhile. They'll work together in their groups to study an assigned Bible story, discussing and

LEADER TIP

If the study groups have more than 10 students each, you may want to have them subdivide into smaller groups. (For example, you might have two groups of six students each studying and discussing the Group 1 Bible stories.)

taking notes on the "Jesus' Radical Love" pages in their Student Journals (pp. 46-47).

Assign groups the following passages:

Group 1: Lepers in Mark 1:40-42 and Luke 17:11-19

Group 2: Zacchaeus in Luke 19:1-10 and Levi in Matthew 9:10-13

Group 3: Samaritan woman in John 4:1-29

LEADER TIP

You may want to mention to Group 1 that those called "lepers" in Scripture may have suffered from any number of skin diseases, not only what is known as leprosy today. Bad rashes, psoriasis, or even bad burns could cause someone to be considered a "leper" and excluded from normal society.

Give groups 15 minutes to study their passages using the study guide in their Student Journals. Warn them when they only have five minutes left. When time is up, explain that each student should pick an object from their group's pile. (It's OK if it's not the original object they brought.) Let students know they'll have some personal time to think seriously about how the object could serve as a representation of Jesus' love. Direct them to turn to page 48 in their Student Journal ("Jesus' Love Object Lesson") to guide their thoughts.

After about five minutes, prompt students to go around their groups, explaining their object lessons by saying, "Jesus' love is like [the object], it…" and completing the sentence. After everybody has shared, the members of each group should work together to decide which object and symbolic description best relates to the scenarios they studied. Let them know that they'll use that object to explain their Bible passages to the rest of the class.

Ask for a representative from each group to present to the rest of the students a short summary of what they studied, what their conclusions were, and how their chosen object symbolizes Jesus' love.

When representatives from each of the three groups have shared, prompt students to return to their original trios and discuss the following question. Ask:

- **What one aspect of your group study and discussion really stood out to you or personally impacted you? Why?**

TRANSFORMATION

Repeat and summarize the main points that groups have shared by saying something like this: **Jesus reached out in love to social outcasts. He touched and healed those with leprosy—people who rarely had any close human contact because of their highly contagious disease. He befriended tax collectors—people considered to be rats, traitors, and swindlers. He showed grace and kindness to sexually promiscuous people. Jesus' love overstepped social boundaries. He saw beyond labels and sinful behaviors; he busted through stereotypes. Jesus' love looked straight to the heart—he saw the unique value of every human being.**

Read aloud this charge to your group, from 1 John 4:7-12, 20-21 in *The Message:* **My beloved friends, let us continue to love each other since love comes from God. Everyone who loves is born of God and experiences a relationship with God. The person who refuses to love doesn't know the first thing about God, because God *is* love—so you can't know him if you don't love.**

This is how God showed his love for us: God sent his only Son into the world so we might live through him. This is the kind of love we are talking about—not that we once upon a time loved God, but that he loved us and sent his Son as a sacrifice to clear away our sins and the damage they've done to our relationship with God. My dear, dear friends, if God loved us like this, we

certainly ought to love each other. No one has seen God, ever. But if we love one another, God dwells deeply within us, and his love becomes complete in us—perfect love!

If anyone boasts "I love God," and goes right on hating his brother or sister, thinking nothing of it, he is a liar. If he won't love the person he can see, how can he love the God he can't see? The command we have from Christ is blunt: Loving God includes loving people. You've got to love both.

Emphasize to students that love is a key distinction of Jesus' kingdom. His is a kingdom in which all are welcomed with open arms! As John explained, our love for God is exhibited in our love for others. It is imperative that Christians imitate Jesus by loving others just as he loved.

Invite a volunteer to read aloud Matthew 11:19, then say: **Jesus was called a friend of sinners because of his kingdom love for all people. He wore this title as a badge of honor. Let's commit to follow his example.**

Hand out the "Hello, My Name Is" adhesive name tags and markers— one name tag per student. Instruct teenagers to write "friend of sinners" on the name tag, then share in their trio one specific action step they'll each take as they grow in showing Jesus' kingdom love to others. After they each share an idea, they should stick their name tag on page 49 in their Student Journal as an act of commitment, symbolizing their desire to follow in Jesus' footsteps and become a friend of sinners.

Conclude by singing (or reading) together four verses of Charles Wesley's hymn *O For a Thousand Tongues to Sing*. Have youth turn to page 49 of their Student Journals; the lyrics are included on page 98 for your convenience. Wesley originally wrote 17 verses for this hymn, though most hymnals only include 4 or 5. Point out to students that these verses (which may be new to them) emphasize God's love and grace for *all* people.

> ## LEADER TIP
>
> Point out the Study 9 "On Your Own" section in the student journals on page 45, and encourage teenagers to use the personal Bible study and reflection suggestions in their devotional time during the week.

O For a Thousand Tongues to Sing

by Charles Wesley (stanzas 7, 14, 15, and 16)

O for a thousand tongues to sing
my great Redeemer's praise!
The glories of my God and King,
the triumphs of his grace.

See all your sins on Jesus laid;
the Lamb of God was slain,
his soul was once an offering made
for every soul of man.

Harlots and publicans and thieves,
in holy triumph join!
Saved is the sinner that believes
from crimes as great as mine.

Murderers and all ye hellish crew,
ye sons of lust and pride,
believe the Savior died for you;
for me the Savior died.

Study 10

The Crucifixion—Jesus as the Lamb

Scripture Focus: Exodus 12:1-11, 21-23; Leviticus 4:32-35; Numbers 28:1-8; Mark 15:6-39; Romans 3:21-26; 1 Corinthians 5:7; 1 Peter 1:18-19

Supplies: Bibles; Student Journals; pens or pencils; several sheets of white poster board, card stock, or regular paper; crayons; markers; easel, tape, or tacks; *City on a Hill: The Gathering* CD or *The Christ: His Passion* CD (optional); CD player (optional); *The Passion of the Christ* DVD or video or *Jesus of Nazareth* DVD or video (optional); DVD player or VCR (optional); TV (optional)

> *"There, where the cross stands, the resurrection is near; even there, where everyone begins to doubt God, where everyone despairs of God's power, there God is whole, there Christ is active and near...Where the power of darkness does violence to the light of God, there God triumphs and judges the darkness." —Dietrich Bonhoeffer, from a sermon in **A Testament to Freedom***

PREPARATION

Before the meeting, read the Leader Insight section to dive deeper into the topic of Jesus' death. Then read through the study to familiarize yourself with the Scripture passages and activities.

For the **Exploration** activity, groups will create storyboards, so you'll need 8½x11 (or larger) pieces of white poster board or card stock. (Regular paper will work also.) You'll also need crayons and colored markers. Students will need an easel to present their storyboards—or you can have them tape (or tack) their papers to the wall.

For the **Transformation** activity, several suggestions incorporate music and video. If you're able, acquire a copy of the *City on a Hill:*

The young, innocent, perfect lamb stands at the center of the Jewish practice of sacrifice; this means that the lamb stood at the center of the Jewish understanding of atonement.

The sound and the sight of the slaughtered lamb were a constant symbol of the covering of sin and God's forgiveness. Every day two lambs would be sacrificed. Each Sabbath another two were laid on the altar. In addition to these, seven lambs would be sacrificed each new moon and seven more at the new year. Also, for each of the first two festivals, the Feast of Unleavened Bread and the Feast of Weeks, seven lambs would be slaughtered. For Yom Kippur, seven more.

Then in autumn, when the farming season came to a close, the Israelites celebrated the third major festival, the Feast of Tabernacles. On this occasion the people were commanded to sacrifice 14 lambs per day for seven days. On the eighth and final day, seven lambs would be sacrificed. These sacrifice requirements can be found in Numbers 28–29.

When John the Baptist proclaimed, "Look, the Lamb of God, who takes away the sin of the world," in essence what the people heard was, "Look, this person will be killed for our sins." Andrew was compelled to follow Jesus. He got his brother and confessed, "We have found the Messiah." In other words, we have found the Anointed One of Isaiah, who would be "led like a lamb to

The Gathering CD (or The Christ: His Passion CD), and set up a CD player so you can play the song "Beautiful Scandalous Night." (There are several other great recordings of this song on other CDs, so if you have a different version, go ahead and use that.) Also, set up a TV and VCR or DVD player. Select a crucifixion scene from the movie The Passion of the Christ or, if you'd prefer something more tame, show the crucifixion scene from Jesus of Nazareth. Youth will watch this scene with the sound on mute, so cue up the video to the scene of your choice and get everything set for when you'll press "Play."

CONNECTION

Warmly welcome students as they arrive, then open the study by telling students that the topic you'll be focusing on is Jesus' death. Ask them to reflect and pray silently for a few minutes, considering the topic and preparing their hearts.

the slaughter." Jesus would be led to the altar of Golgotha as a sacrifice, but he would not be led against his will (John 10:18). And slaughter! That word proves all too accurate—more so than Andrew or any of the disciples could have anticipated.

The Apostle Paul, who at one point had fiercely defended the ritual of sacrifice as a Pharisee and who, no doubt, supported the crucifixion of Jesus, would eventually come to realize how the two would merge. About a quarter of a century after the slaughter had taken place (A.D. 57), Paul was completing his third and final missionary journey. At that time he wrote to the house churches in Rome, "God presented [Jesus] as a *sacrifice of atonement*" (Romans 3:25, emphasis added). Here we see that Paul takes the ritual that has symbolized God's mercy and the covering of sins for so long and presents Jesus as the ultimate sacrifice that atones for all sin, once and for all.

In 1 Corinthians 5:7, Paul calls Jesus "our Passover lamb." Although his concern in this passage is the removal of sin from the community of believers, it reveals a second important role of Christ's crucifixion in the mind of Paul. Jesus is the Passover lamb, the means of salvation from bondage.

When we combine Paul's first idea of Christ as the sacrificial lamb with his idea of Jesus as the Passover lamb, we find that the two join to form two sides of the same coin, atonement and salvation. And so it is: Jesus is the Lamb of God.

Allow the room to become starkly silent. After a couple of minutes, say: **While the sun was still rising in the eastern sky over the crowded streets of Jerusalem, a bloodied and bent man carried a wooden beam. It was the day before the Sabbath. On this sacred day lambs would be sacrificed as a way of "covering" the sins of the people. It was also the week of Passover, a time of the year when pilgrims would visit the crown city of Judah, and lambs would be sacrificed as a remembrance of the Passover event in Egypt. God delivered his people from slavery, striking down the firstborn of every household in Egypt, passing over and sparing only those whose homes were marked with lamb's blood over the door frames.**

These two holy observances place the perfect and innocent lamb at the center of the people's forgiveness and salvation. And so, the Son of God, beaten beyond recognition, "was led like a

lamb to the slaughter" (Isaiah 53:7). **Contrary to how it appeared to many observers, however, his life was not *taken* from him—he laid it down by his own accord** (John 10:18).

Ask:

- **What thoughts, images, and ideas come to mind when you hear Isaiah's description, "He was led like a lamb to the slaughter"?**

- **A simile is a figure of speech used to compare two ideas using *like* or *as* to paint a more vivid picture. He was led *like* a lamb to the slaughter. What is the power of the simile in this passage from Isaiah?**

Why do you think Isaiah used this word picture for Jesus? What does it mean?

Say: **Jesus' death is arguably the most famous in the world. It is commemorated every Good Friday. People wear the symbol of his execution—a cross—around their necks, as earrings, and even as a popular tattoo design. But what lies behind all these images? Today we're going to learn about Jesus' death by looking more closely at the power in the image Isaiah painted—Jesus as the lamb led to the slaughter.**

EXPLORATION

Divide the group into two teams and explain that each team is going to study an Old Testament perspective on lambs.

Assign one group to study the Passover lamb, focusing on Exodus 12:1-11, 21-23.

Assign the other group to study lambs used in sacrifices, focusing on Leviticus 4:32-35 and Numbers 28:1-8.

Let students know that they'll have about 20 minutes to study their verses, discuss them together, and then create storyboards that they'll use to teach their

LEADER TIP

You may want to spend time with each group, making sure students understand the context and purpose of the Passover lamb and the regular sacrifices of lambs to atone for sins. Consider sharing with students the information you've gleaned from the Leader Insight section.

passage to the other team. Direct students to turn to pages 52-53 in their Student Journals, where they'll find discussion questions, tips, and instructions for creating storyboards and creative presentation ideas.

Answer any questions students might have, and let them get started. While they're working, circulate between groups to ensure that their storyboards and presentations will be done in the allotted time frame.

Give teams a five-minute warning, then when time is up call everyone back together and invite teams to present their storyboards and conclusions to each other. Applaud both teams' efforts, then have youth form new small groups of three or four, making sure that there

LEADER TIP

If you have more than 20 students, form four teams. By keeping storyboard teams to 10 students or fewer, you'll ensure that all team members are able to be involved in the creation of the storyboards. Assign two of the teams the "Passover Lamb" assignment and the other two the "Sacrificial Lamb" assignment. When they're done preparing their storyboards, have teams pair up so that each Passover Lamb team presents their conclusions to a Sacrificial Lamb team and vice versa.

are representatives of each storyboard team in each new small group.

Direct small groups to read 1 Corinthians 5:7 and 1 Peter 1:18-19 and discuss these questions. Ask:

- **Why is Jesus called "the Passover lamb"?**
- **How were his life and death like those of the Passover lamb? How were they different?**
- **What meaning does this add to your understanding of Jesus' death?**
- **Why is Jesus compared to the sacrificial lambs?**
- **How were his life and death like those of the sacrificial lambs? How were they different?**
- **What meaning does this add to your understanding of Jesus' death?**

Direct small groups to read aloud together the "Definitions of Terms" box in their Student Journals on page 53.

For your convenience, here are the definitions included in the Student Journal:

Righteousness of God: God's faithfulness to carry out his plan of salvation for us through Jesus.

Justified: Acquitted of guilt; declared innocent from the charge of sin.

Redemption: Set free through the payment of a debt; ransomed.

Sacrifice of atonement: The removal of sin and the turning away of God's wrath through the sacrifice of Jesus.

Once everybody is clear on the meaning of each term, direct small groups to read Romans 3:21-26 and discuss these questions. Ask:

- **What verse or phrase sticks out to you the most from this passage? Why?**
- **What is Paul really saying here? What does Jesus' death mean?**

TRANSFORMATION

Gather everyone back together and invite small groups to share what they discussed. Then say: **As we learned earlier, Isaiah prophesied that Jesus would be "led like a lamb to the slaughter," but Isaiah wasn't the only prophet to refer to Jesus in this way. John the Baptist declared in John 1:29, "Look, the Lamb of God, who takes away the sin of the world!"**

Invite youth to turn to a partner and share one way that what they've learned about lambs and their significance alters or impacts their personal understanding of Jesus' death.

Ask students to silently pray again as they listen to the words of a song, considering how Jesus lovingly

> **LEADER TIP**
>
> Just a reminder that in Study 12, you'll need to pass out a bunch of newspapers from a variety of dates, so keep collecting them (or if you haven't started yet, start now).

sacrificed himself to atone for their sins. Play the song "Beautiful Scandalous Night" from the *City on a Hill: The Gathering* CD ········

Then have students gather around the TV and open their Bibles to Mark 15:6-39. Begin to play the crucifixion scene you selected, making sure the TV is on mute. While the scene is playing, slowly go through the Scripture passage aloud, either reading it yourself or having student volunteers read.

When you're done reading the passage, allow youth to watch about one more minute of the video while it is silent. Then turn off the TV and ask:

- **What are your reactions to Jesus' death and what it means?**
- **What are your thoughts, questions, feelings?**
- **What is your response to the cross?**

After several students have shared, invite everyone to turn to page 55 in their Student Journals, where they'll find the text of the hymn "When I Survey the Wondrous Cross." The lyrics are printed on page 106 for your convenience. Explain that this song represents Isaac Watts' own reflections and feelings when he considered Jesus' death on the cross for his sins. Have the group read the lyrics aloud, directing individual students to take turns reading lines. Have students go around the circle or down each row, continuing until the whole song has been read.

NON-MEDIA OPTION

If you're unable to play the song "Beautiful Scandalous Night," then skip ahead directly to the student reading of Mark 15:6-39. Also, if you're unable to show a video depiction of the Crucifixion on mute during the reading, that's OK—the Scripture passage is extremely powerful and moving on its own! Just have students read the passage and use their imaginations, picturing the events as they occur. Or, if your church has paintings or other replicas of the cross, put those in the front of the room and ask students to focus on them as they listen to the reading.

After the song, share with students which phrase from the song stands out to you the most and why. Then say: **In our very first study, we considered that the Old Testament prophesied a Messiah who'd be a servant and a king. Two weeks ago we learned about the value Jesus placed on serving others. Yet nothing exemplifies Jesus as** a servant better than his willingness to go to the cross, to be "led like a lamb to the slaughter." Matthew 20:28 records Jesus' words, saying "The Son of Man did not come to be served, but to serve, and to give his life as a ransom for many."

Lead the students in a concluding prayer.

When I Survey the Wondrous Cross
by Isaac Watts

When I survey the wondrous cross on which the Prince of glory died,

My richest gain I count but loss, and pour contempt on all my pride.

Forbid it, Lord, that I should boast save in the death of Christ, my God.

All the vain things that charm me most, I sacrifice them to his blood.

See, from his head, his hands, his feet, sorrow and love flow mingled down.

Did e'er such love and sorrow meet or thorns compose so rich a crown?

Were the whole realm of nature mine, that were an offering far too small;

Love so amazing, so divine, demands my soul, my life, my all.

LEADER TIP

Point out the Study 10 "On Your Own" section in the student journals on page 51, and encourage teenagers to use the personal Bible study and reflection suggestions in their devotional time during the week.

The Resurrection—Jesus Conquers Death

Scripture Focus: John 19:31–20:18; Acts 2:24; 1 Corinthians 15:3-7, 12-19; 1 Peter 1:3
Supplies: Bibles; Student Journals; pens or pencils; a copy of *Bambi—A Life in the Woods* by Felix Salten (optional); 1 copy of your church's creed or statement of faith regarding the Resurrection; 8 newsprint banners; markers; art supplies such as glitter, yarn, crayons, paint, feathers, or sequins; tacks or tape; CD of reflective Christian music or instrumental music (optional); CD player (optional)

> *"Easter gives the next piece of the story begun at Christmas and continued into Good Friday. He lived for us and then He died for us and then He rose for us. His death atoned for our sins and His resurrection opens the door to everlasting life."* —Lauren F. Winner, **Girl Meets God**

PREPARATION

Before the meeting, read the Leader Insight section to dive deeper into the topic of Jesus' resurrection. Then read through the study to familiarize yourself with the Scripture passages and activities.

For the **Connection** activity, try to obtain a copy of the book *Bambi—A Life in the Woods* by Felix Salten so you can read an excerpt from the start of chapter eight. This is a classic children's book and is available to be checked out at most libraries. It is also available for sale at most major bookstores. (If you're unable to locate this book, another option is included on pages 109-110.)

For the **Transformation** activity, you'll need eight newsprint banners and a variety of art supplies students can use to write on

When Peter stood up in Jerusalem on the day of Pentecost and proclaimed, "God has raised this Jesus to life" (Acts 2:32), he was saying a new thing. The ancients of the Greco-Roman world did not believe in bodily resurrection, and the Jewish people believed it had simply not happened yet. To be raised back to life was a new claim; no one had succeeded in frustrated attempts at attaining this hope, victory over death. Death had always stared humanity down—never flinching and always insistent.

The prevailing ideas concerning life after death in the Roman world varied from Homer's gloom, where the self is composed only of physical matter and the dead carry out a meaningless existence, to Plato's affirmation of the soul and life after death. Between these views lay the Stoics, who believed that death is a separation of the body and the soul. The Stoic philosopher, Seneca, believed that the preexistent soul would return home to the stars.

The most basic concept is summed up well by N.T. Wright in *The Resurrection of the Son of God:* "Who were the dead thought to be in the ancient pagan world? They were beings that had once been embodied human beings, but were now souls...Where were they? Most likely in Hades; possibly in the Isles of the Blessed."

and decorate those banners. You'll also need tape or tacks that students can use to hang the banners around the room. In addition, obtain a copy of your church's own creed or statement of faith regarding the Resurrection that you can give to one of the groups. The Transformation section also includes a journaling activity during which you may want to play some background music such as an instrumental CD or a reflective Christian album. If you choose this option, set up the CD player and CD so you'll just need to hit "Play."

CONNECTION

Greet students as they arrive, and launch the study by having students gather around for a "story time." If you're able to borrow or buy a copy of the book *Bambi—A Life in the Woods* by Felix Salten, read to students the first two pages of chapter eight, stopping after the first leaf says, "Who knows? Not one of all those down there has ever come back to tell us about it."

Reincarnation even snuck into the mix in some worldviews. But, as Wright concludes, life after death in the ancient world is best characterized as a "one-way street." No popular worldview concerning life after death in the Greco-Roman world included the idea that one could, or has, come back from death.

Though the Jewish people did not believe that anyone had actually been raised from the dead before the time of Jesus, it remained their hope and belief that one day death would be defeated. Daniel 12:2-3 speaks of "multitudes who sleep in the dust of the earth will awake." Isaiah 26:19 says, "But your dead will live; their bodies will rise." And Hosea 13:14 reads, "I will ransom them from the power of the grave; I will redeem them from death."

When Christianity came along, it claimed an entirely new thing. It stood apart. The resurrection of Jesus stood apart, and it stands distinct today from all the other systems of belief. God became man, suffered, died, was buried, and was bodily raised back to life. Sin and death were conquered. As G.K. Chesterton wrote in *The Everlasting Man*, "Christianity, appearing amid heathen humanity, had all the character of a unique thing...It was not like any of the other things; and the more we study it the less it looks like any of them."

If you're not able to locate the book, read this summary and short excerpt to the group. Say: **In the book *Bambi—A Life in the Woods* by Felix Salten, we come across a conversation between two leaves in a tree. It is autumn and the leaves are beginning to dry up and fall off of the trees. The two leaves in this conversation are wondering what will happen to them when they fall off the tree onto the forest floor. They're sad, afraid, and curious about the mystery of death. Here's part of their conversation:**

The second leaf asked, "What happens to us when we have fallen?"

"We sink down..."

..."Do we feel anything, do we know anything about ourselves when we're down there?"

The first leaf answered, "Who knows? Not one of all those down there has ever come back to tell us about it."

Ask:

- **How is this conversation between the leaves similar to the way many people think and feel regarding death?**
- **Do most people fear death? Why or why not?**
- **What are some of the most commonly held beliefs about what happens after death?**

Explain to students the most commonly held beliefs about death during the time of Jesus; you'll find this information in the Leader Insight section on pages 108-109. Invite them to comment on those views: How do they compare and contrast with contemporary views of death and the afterlife? Then ask:

- **How do you think Jesus' followers felt after he died? What might they have thought?**

EXPLORATION

Say: **Near the end of the first century, John wrote his gospel for a wide audience. Imagine this is your first exposure to the story of Jesus—you've never heard about this man before. And like the two leaves, what happens after death remains unknown to you. Listen to this account with fresh ears.**

Invite volunteers to read aloud John 19:31–20:18, then have students discuss these questions with a partner. Ask:

- **If you lived in Jesus' time and heard someone tell this account, what would your reaction be? Why?**
- **What would it mean to you that someone had risen from the dead?**

Say: **Let's look at this resurrection account from our perspective today.**

Prompt youth to form groups of three or four, and have them turn to the "To Believe or Not to Believe" section in their Student Journals on page 58. (This page in the Student Journal helps teenagers consider the implications of a person's viewpoint if that person does *not* believe in the Resurrection.) Instruct them to take a few minutes to write their own notes, thoughts, and answers to the questions, then to discuss the questions together in their small groups.

After 10 to 15 minutes, invite small groups to share what they discussed, then say: **The Apostle Paul wrote that if Jesus hadn't truly risen from the dead, the Christian faith is pointless.**

Have a volunteer read aloud 1 Corinthians 15:12-19. Ask:

- **Do you agree with Paul? Why or why not?**
- **Why is faith in Jesus' resurrection an absolutely essential component of Christianity?**

TRANSFORMATION

Have teenagers form eight groups of at least two students each. (If you have fewer than 16 students, simply eliminate one or more of the "confessions" from this activity.) Prompt students to turn to "Christian Confessions" on pages 59-60 in their Student Journals, where they'll find a listing of seven historical Christian creeds and quotes that affirm the Resurrection. (For your convenience, each of the creeds is included on page 113.) Assign one quote to each group and assign the final group a copy of your church's own creed or statement of faith regarding the Resurrection. Give each group a banner, marker, and art supplies.

LEADER TIP

To make the banners durable and long-lasting, have teenagers create them on large sheets of white fabric and write with fabric markers, puffy paint, and other craft supplies. Then you can use them to decorate your youth room or church for years to come!

Tell groups that you'd like them to copy their quotes onto their banners and then decorate them in any way they'd like. Encourage them to be creative as they work together using pictures, symbols, and other visual decorations to make their banner unique and beautiful. Give groups 10 to 15 minutes to create their banners, then have them hang the banners around the room.

When all the banners are hung, compliment students on their great work. Then invite someone from each group to read the group's quote or creed aloud.

Ask:

- **Why is this belief that Jesus rose from the dead such a central part of all these confessions of Christian faith, spanning many denominations and centuries?**
- **What is unique about your creed?**
- **How does Jesus' resurrection distinguish Christianity from all other religions? Explain.**

Then say: **All Christians celebrate the fact of the Resurrection. For over 2,000 years and across denominational lines, Jesus' resurrection has remained the essence of what makes Christianity *Christianity*. Jesus' resurrection proved true his claim to be the Son of God. As Peter said at Pentecost, "It was impossible for death to keep its hold on him" (Acts 2:24). Our belief in the resurrection affects everything—our faith, our view of Jesus, and our thoughts and feelings about death. Because Jesus conquered death, what happens after we have "fallen from the tree" doesn't have to remain a mystery to us. Someone has come back from the dead to tell us about it!**

 Have students turn to "Implications of the Resurrection" in their Student Journals (p. 61) and take five minutes to journal their thoughts. Play some meditative or reflective music while students write.

Conclude by leading the group in praying 1 Peter 1:3 together, saying: **"Praise be to the God and Father of our Lord Jesus Christ! In his great mercy he has given us new birth into a living hope through the resurrection of Jesus Christ from the dead."**

LEADER TIP

Point out the Study 11 "On Your Own" section in the Student Journals on page 57, and encourage teenagers to use the personal Bible study and reflection suggestions in their devotional time during the week.

Christian Confessions

1. "For what I received I passed on to you as of first importance: that Christ died for our sins according to the Scriptures, that he was buried, that he was raised on the third day according to the Scriptures, and that he appeared to Peter, and then to the Twelve. After that, he appeared to more than five hundred of the brothers at the same time, most of whom are still living, though some have fallen asleep. Then he appeared to James, then to all the apostles." —the Apostle Paul in 1 Corinthians 15:3-7 (approximately A.D. 55)

2. "The third day [Jesus] arose again from the dead. He ascended into heaven and sits at the right hand of God the Father Almighty, whence He shall come to judge the living and the dead…[I believe in] the resurrection of the body, and life everlasting. Amen." —the Apostles' Creed (late second century)

3. "[The Church believes] in one Jesus Christ, the Son of God, who became incarnate for our salvation…and the resurrection from the dead, and the ascension into heaven in the flesh of the beloved Christ Jesus, our Lord." —Irenaeus (A.D.190)

4. "[We believe] that this [Son] was sent by the Father into the virgin and was born of her both man and God, Son of man and Son of God, and was named Jesus Christ: that he suffered, died, and was buried, according to the scriptures, and, having been raised up by the Father and taken back into heaven, sits at the right hand of the Father." —Tertullian (A.D. 200)

5. "We believe in…one Lord Jesus Christ, the Son of God, begotten of the Father as only begotten…He suffered and the third day he rose, and ascended into the heavens." —the Nicene Creed (A.D. 325)

6. "[Christ] rose from the dead on the third day, ascended into heaven, and sits on the right hand of God, that he may eternally rule and have dominion over all creatures." —the Augsburg Confession (A.D. 1530)

7. "[Jesus] endured most grievous torments immediately in his soul, and most painful suffering in his body; was crucified, and died; was buried, and remained under the power of death, yet saw no corruption. On the third day he arose from the dead, with the same body in which he suffered." —the Westminster Confession of Faith (A.D. 1646)

The Reign of Christ

••

Scripture Focus: Revelation 5:1–6:1; 7:9, 10, 14, 17; 12:11; 13:8; 14:1, 10; 15:3; 17:14; 19:7, 9; 21:1–22:21

Supplies: Bibles; Student Journals; pens or pencils; index cards; masking tape; newspapers (see Preparation section on pages 115-116); scissors; markers; outdoor fire pit, large metal garbage can, or large metal coffee can (optional); kindling (optional); matches (optional); guitar, piano, or other musical instruments (optional); lyrics and music for favorite praise songs (optional); Chris Tomlin's *Arriving* CD (optional); CD player (optional)

••

> "If there's anyone who can appear before Aslan without their knees knocking, they're either braver than most or else just silly." "Then he isn't safe?" said Lucy. "Safe?" said Mr. Beaver…"Who said anything about safe? 'Course he isn't safe. But he's good. He's the King, I tell you."
>
> —C.S. Lewis, **The Lion, the Witch and the Wardrobe**

PREPARATION

Before the meeting, read the Leader Insight section to dive deeper into the topic of Jesus' return. Then read through the study to familiarize yourself with the Scripture passages and activities.

For the **Connection** activity, you'll need 2 index cards per student, along with 6-10 additional index cards. On the extra index cards, write the names of animals such as dog, cat, llama, giraffe, alligator, tiger, dolphin, turtle, eagle, or butterfly. Also tear several small pieces of tape, two or three per student.

For the **Exploration** section, you'll need a collection of newspapers.

The concepts of judgment and hope are twin pillars of Old Testament theology. Two different and great examples of this are the books of Isaiah and Amos. Interspersed in the judgment passages of Isaiah is found a hope of "newness." The people are commanded to sing a new song (Isaiah 42:10), new things are being declared and done (Isaiah 42:9; 43:19), the people will be called by a new name (Isaiah 62:2), and a new heaven and a new earth will be created (Isaiah 65:17). In Isaiah we see a hope for the people, which is found in the prophesied servant.

In Amos, the prophet rattles off oracles of judgment at a rapid pace, one after another, until the end, where Amos offers restoration to the people of God. David's tent will be repaired, the farmland will be replenished with a harvest, the ruined cities will be rebuilt, and the people replanted in their land forever (Amos 9:11-15). Just as the Old Testament speaks of God's judgment upon his people and the nations before turning to God's hope for all the nations (the "nations will stream to [Zion]" in Isaiah 2:2),

It is best if they are papers from the last several weeks or months; this will ensure that they contain a variety of stories and features. Also, think about and prepare to share a personal story of pain or tragedy, such as the death of a loved one, an illness that afflicted a friend, or something else that has been emotionally painful.

For the **Transformation** activity, you'll need to set up an outdoor "fire pit" area. You may have access to a fire pit that already exists. If not, consider creating one in an area that is just dirt or stone. Dig a small pit, surround it with stones, and prepare kindling for a small fire. (Make sure you are not in an area where hot ash could be picked up by wind and land on flammable material.) Or you could create an imitation "fire pit" by using a large metal garbage can or a large metal coffee can. Put kindling in the can and set it in an area that is far away from grass, trees, or other flammable material.

The study concludes with a time of worship singing, so grab your guitar (or other instrument) and a few of your students' favorite praise songs. The song "How Great Is Our God" by Chris Tomlin would be a perfect conclusion to lead the group in singing together; if you don't so too does Revelation offer this reality of judgment and hope. They are inseparable.

In Revelation 5, the Lamb is the only one found who can open the scroll. The opening of the scroll sets into motion the final stages of God's judgment upon the earth. Finally, "the Kingdom of the world has become the kingdom of our Lord and of his Christ" (Revelation 11:15). Consistent with the general theme of all prophecy concerning the last days, the judgment necessarily precedes the hope. And that is the point: Revelation is ultimately a book of hope, promising redemption and life.

George Eldon Ladd states it succinctly and well in *A Theology of the New Testament:* "The coming of God's kingdom is pictured in two-toned colors: the destruction of evil and the blessing of eternal life." This is precisely the reason why the Lamb overtakes the image of the Lion. The "destruction of evil" and "the blessing of eternal life" were gained on the cross. The Lamb is the victor over sin and death; the Lion reigns as a result.

---

know how to play the song, you may want to set up a CD player to play the song from Tomlin's CD *Arriving* and lead students in singing along. If your group doesn't like to sing together, a non-musical worship option is also included.

CONNECTION

Start things out with a fun mixer. Distribute two index cards per student and pencils or pens, and have youth anonymously write down their answer to the question: **If you were an animal, what would you be?** Direct students to pick two animals that best match two aspects of their personality (one per card).

When they're done writing, collect the cards, add in the cards you prepared before the study, and mix them all up. Then redistribute the cards so everyone has two, and give everyone a few pieces of masking tape. Lay the remaining cards in a pile at the front of the room.

Tell teenagers to read their cards, then let them know they'll have five minutes to mingle around and tape each card to the back of a person whose personality they think best matches the animal on the card.

Here are the rules:

- The goal is that at the end of the five minutes, both cards a player holds must be taped to others' backs. Also, by the end of five minutes, every player must have a minimum of two cards taped to his or her own back.

- Students may not look at a card that's taped on their own back nor can they ask others about the card on their own back.

- Each student is allowed one "switch"—teenagers can trade one of their cards with one from the pile of extra cards you set at the front of the room.

Ask if there are any questions, then let the students get started. Give them a warning when there's only one minute left, prompting them to make sure that every player has at least two cards on his or her back.

When time is up, have everybody gather back together, take the cards off their backs, and read them. Form groups of three or four and prompt teenagers to discuss these questions. Ask:

- **Are you surprised by the two animals others associated with your personality? Why or why not?**

- **Do you agree that the animals taped to your back are a fit for you?**

- **What aspects of your personality do the animals taped to your back define for you?**

- **What two animals did you originally write down? How do these animals define you?**

Say: **In the last book in the Bible, Revelation, animals are used symbolically. In chapter 5, John sees two different animals in a vision. Let's look at these animals and consider why we think they appear in John's vision.**

LEADER TIP

If students aren't familiar with the concept of Jesus' Second Coming, refer them to John 14:1-4, where Jesus promises his followers that he is preparing a place for them and will return for them. Also have them check out Acts 1:11, where an angel tells Jesus' disciples that he will one day return in the sky.

EXPLORATION

Explain to youth that the book of Revelation was written by the Apostle John toward the end of his life. It describes a vision given to him by God about the end times and Jesus' return.

Invite a volunteer to read aloud Revelation 5:2-10 while everyone else reads along in their own Bibles, then ask small groups:

- **What animals were used to describe Jesus?**
- **What are the traits of a lion?**
- **How are those traits meant to apply to Jesus?**
- **What are the traits of a lamb?**
- **How are they meant to apply to Jesus?**
- **What is the relationship between verse 5 and verse 6?**

Explain that this description of Jesus is a paradox—two seemingly contradictory images that are both true. Whereas lions are fierce, deadly, powerful, and recognized as the king of the jungle; lambs are meek, innocent, peaceful, and meant for sacrifice. Help students discover that in verse 5, John is instructed to see the Lion who has triumphed. Yet when he looks (verse 6), he sees the Lamb that was slain. Jesus' triumph and kingly rule is inextricably tied to—in fact is a *result of*—his sacrifice and death as the Lamb.

Say: **Let's read some more descriptions of Jesus in John's vision.**

Assign students to read aloud these verses, quickly going from one verse to the next: Revelation 7:9; 7:10; 7:14; 7:17; 12:11; 13:8; 14:1; 14:10; 15:3; 17:14; 19:7; 19:9; 21:9; 21:22; 21:23; 21:27; 22:1; and 22:3.

After the litany of verses, say: **As you noticed, the most dominant image of Jesus in the book of Revelation is "the Lamb of God."**

Ask: **Why do you think this image of Jesus is the most dominant in Revelation?**

Invite students to share their thoughts, then say: **In Revelation 5:5 Jesus is depicted as a lion, the king of the universe; yet he is king because he was first the lamb—the "Lamb of God, who takes away the sin of the world"** (John 1:29). **Revelation calls Jesus "the Lamb" 28 times, emphasizing this critical fact: Death, evil, and sin have been defeated through Jesus' sacrifice.**

One day this truth will be realized for us in the new heaven and earth. (Pause.) **But for now, death, evil, hurt, and sin are prevalent in our world.**

Distribute the newspapers you've collected to your small groups, along with scissors and markers. Direct the groups to take up to 10 minutes to look through the newspapers and cut out articles that demonstrate the pervasiveness of evil, sin, pain, and death in our world. (For example, teenagers may cut out articles about crime, terrorism, depression, drug use, disease, or even obituaries.) Have teenagers circle key words and phrases that emphasize the evil or emotional pain in each article. As groups select articles, they should tape them on a designated wall in the room. When time's up, direct everyone to tour the wall, quietly looking at the various articles and reading the key words.

LEADER TIP

As you share openly and honestly with students about difficult situations or emotions you've dealt with, you're helping them form a healthy understanding of Christian faith. Sometimes hurting teenagers wonder, "Do other Christians ever feel this way? Does this mean I have a weak faith?" Your vulnerability will encourage them to press on in faith when they face tough times.

When everyone has gathered back together, gesture toward the articles and say: **This is the world we live in. Though we'd often like to ignore it or deny it, the truth is that this world is full of evil, pain, sin, and death. Tragedy and hurt will strike all of our lives eventually.**

Take a moment to share openly and honestly with students about a time evil, sin, pain, or death impacted your life—such as the pain you experienced when a friend or parent died, the challenge of seeing a loved one face a disease, or your thoughts and feelings regarding a recent occurrence of terrorism, war, or crime.

When you've finished sharing, instruct students to silently reflect on something painful from their own lives—to remember when the sin of this world hurt them or a loved one.

Then say: **Let's continue to study John's vision.**

Have the students return to Revelation 5 in their Bibles, and ask a volunteer to read aloud Revelation 5:1-4.

Ask: **Why does John weep?**

Allow students to answer; if they need help, prompt them to examine the passage to discover that John weeps because no one was found who was able to open the scroll.

Then have a few more volunteers read aloud Revelation 5:5–6:1.

Say: **The scroll must be opened because it signals the beginning of God's final judgment; it is this judgment that opens the way for the hope of all humankind to become reality. Only he who defeated death on the cross wields the power to set into motion this final cascade of events that leads to the climax of all human history. The defeat of evil, death, and sin is finally near when the Lamb opens the first seal and one of the four living creatures says in a thundering voice, "Come!"**

If no one were able to open the seal, evil and death would reign forever and all hope would be lost for humankind. It is because of the Lamb's victory on the cross that he is able to open the scroll.

Direct students to look again at the montage of evil, death, and pain symbolized in the newspaper clippings on the walls.

Repeat: **If no one were able to open the seal, evil and death would reign forever and all hope would be lost for humankind.**

Then say: **But, that is not the case. There *is* one who is able to open the scroll. This means that all our deepest longings will one day be met. Evil, death, and sin will be defeated. Imagine: no more death, evil, suffering, or pain! Imagine: only everlasting joy!**

Invite volunteers to read aloud Revelation 21:1–22:21, alternating verses. Then have everyone discuss these questions within their small groups. Ask:

- **What's your initial emotional response when you read about and listen to these awesome descriptions of Jesus' power and glory?**

- **How does this passage describe the new Jerusalem? What are the "best parts" of it, in your opinion?**

- How does this passage describe Jesus? What is his role in the new Jerusalem?

- What does Jesus say in this passage? Which phrase stands out to you the most? Why?

- The first readers of this letter from John were Christians who were being severely persecuted. What hope do you think this vision of the new Jerusalem gave to them?

- What hope does this vision give to you today? Why?

- How does it affect you when you consider that Jesus is the King who reigns on the throne?

TRANSFORMATION

Gather everyone back together and repeat the text of Revelation 21:3-4, saying: **"Now the dwelling of God is with men, and he will live with them. They will be his people, and God himself will be with them and be their God. He will wipe every tear from their eyes. There will be no more death or mourning or crying or pain, for the old order of things has passed away."**

Direct teenagers to tear down the pieces of newspaper on the walls and follow you outside to the "fire pit" area you prepared before the study, bringing their Bibles with them. Have everyone gather around the fire pit and wad up the newspapers. Say: **When Jesus returns, he'll be victorious over sin and death.**

Take one of the wadded-up pieces of newspaper, stuff it into the fire pit with the pieces of kindling you collected, then light it on fire. Tell teenagers to toss their pieces of newspaper into the fire one at a time, symbolizing Jesus' ultimate victory over sin and death. (If smoke or ash are a problem, have teenagers stand away from the fire pit, walking forward one at a time to burn their newspaper articles.) While students are putting their papers in the fire, again read aloud Revelation 22:12-21.

When all the papers have been burned, return to your original meeting room. Remind students of the main themes they've learned from each lesson in this series. You may want to say: **We worship Jesus because he is worthy of worship. He came to earth and was born as a human baby because of his love for us. He was baptized by**

John and started his ministry, calling the disciples to follow him. He displayed power and authority over nature, over illness, over demons. He taught about the kingdom of God—a kingdom of love and servanthood. He willingly died on the cross as the Lamb of God who takes away the

OPTION

If you're unable to burn the newspapers in a fire-safe area, instead have teenagers one at a time tear their newspapers into tiny pieces and toss them in a garbage can (or use a paper shredder). Let them know that this action symbolizes Jesus' triumph over sin and death, and read aloud Revelation 22:12-21 again while they tear their papers.

sins of the world. On the third day, he rose again! And some day, he will return to earth as the fulfillment of all our hope. Jesus will defeat sin and death once and for all and will take us to worship him in joy and delight forever. The only true response to Jesus and his amazing love is to worship him. He is worthy of our praise!

Lead the students in worshipping God by singing some of their favorite praise songs. If you're able, lead the group in singing "How Great Is Our God." If you can't play the song or are unable to locate sheet music, you could play the song on the CD *Arriving* and lead the students in singing along. Or, if your group doesn't sing together or you're unable to lead music, instead invite students to close with a "popcorn" prayer, spontaneously shouting out (or saying) words of praise to God.

Then conclude the study by having the group stand up and read in unison the praise of the angels and heavenly creatures in Revelation 5:12, saying: **Worthy is the Lamb, who was slain, to receive power and wealth and wisdom and strength and honor and glory and praise!** (Students can find this printed on page 64 of their Student Journals if they need help.) Repeat the phrase over and over again, getting louder each time, until the group is virtually shouting it in praise to God, then say: **Amen!**

LEADER TIP

Point out the Study 12 "On Your Own" section in the Student Journals on page 63 and encourage teenagers to use the personal Bible study and reflection suggestions in their devotional time during the week.

EVALUATION FOR
Jesus—The Life Changer: Leader Guide

Please help Group Publishing, Inc., continue to provide innovative and useful resources for ministry. Please take a moment to fill out this evaluation and mail or fax it to us. Thanks!

Group Publishing, Inc.
Attention: Product Development
P.O. Box 481
Loveland, CO 80539
Fax: (970) 292-4370

1. As a whole, this book has been (circle one)
   not very helpful   *very helpful*
   1   2   3   4   5   6   7   8   9   10

2. The best things about this book:

3. Ways this book could be improved:

4. Things I will change because of this book:

5. Other books I'd like to see Group publish in the future:

6. Would you be interested in field-testing future Group products and giving us your feedback? If so, please fill in the information below:

Name_____

Church Name _____

Denomination _____ Church Size _____

Church Address _____

City _____ State _____ ZIP _____

Church Phone_____

E-mail _____

the

1

thing™

that everyone craves.

that really matters.

that gets undivided attention.

that can transform your life.

that encourages pastors.

that will re-energize you.

that will bring you joy.

that will unite your community.

that brings families closer.

that frees you.

that gives you focus.

that answers the why's.

that means true success.

that eliminates distractions.

that gives you real purpose.

that can transform your church.

Discover how *The 1 Thing* can revolutionize the way you approach ministry. It's engaging. Fun. Even shocking. But most of all, it's about re-thinking what "growing a relationship with Jesus" really means. Pick up Thom & Joani Schultz's inspiring new book today.